SOCIAL $ECURITY

ESSENTIALS

SOCIAL SECURITY
ESSENTIALS

Smart Ways to Help BOOST
Your Retirement Income

DEAN BARBER, RFC
AND JOE ELSASSER, CFP®

Financial planning and navigating the many Social Security options and strategies can be very complex. Such planning can be made even more difficult due to the inevitable changes in our personal circumstances and the ever-changing rules and regulations surrounding these topics. Due to these possible changes, the information herein is subject to change.

The examples provided throughout this book are hypothetical in nature and are intended for informational purposes only. They reflect the opinions of the authors and are subject to their own limitations. These opinions are not intended to provide specific advice and should not be construed as recommendations for any individual. This book is published with the understanding that the authors are not engaged in the rendering of legal or tax services. The services of competent legal and tax professionals should be sought prior to executing any strategy.

Investments involve risk including the potential for loss of the principal amount invested. Please remember the financial and investment decisions should be based on an individual's goals, time horizon, and tolerance for risk.

No names of actual clients or their financial situations are revealed. The examples and names here are just for illustration.

Paperback ISBN: 978-0-9899284-1-0

Kindle ISBN: 978-0-9899284-0-3

ePub ISBN: 978-0-9899284-2-7

LCCN: 2013949642

Library of Congress Cataloging Information on file with publisher

10 9 8 7 6 5 4 3 2 1

Contents

FOREWORD
by Lloyd Watnik

I have read many books about Social Security and financial planning. The vast majority of the publications did not fully understand Social Security benefits and how they work.

This book clearly explains the relationship of planning and receiving Social Security benefits. It is completely accurate about Social Security and the choices available to you as of the date of publication. Through examples, it guides you through the jungle that the relationship between Social Security and planning has become.

Since the year 2000, there have been many changes in options for selecting the correct month to start benefits or switch benefits from your benefit as a spouse to your own Social Security benefit. The authors fully understand the options now available through Social Security to select the best benefits and the optimal timing of them.

The examples in this book are the kinds of scenarios I run into on almost a daily basis. The authors' explanations are clear and easy to understand. The technical jargon that Social Security uses is made into everyday language you can understand and appreciate.

The authors give simple advice that can help prolong a successful retirement for years. With this advice in hand, you will know whether your financial advisor understands the benefits and is leading you down the right path to maximizing your retirement benefits.

I have read many books about retirement that give advice about the interaction of Social Security benefits, financial planning, and taxes. If you want my advice, start with this one.

Lloyd Watnik
Social Security Administration
Regional Manager (Retired)
Government Benefits Consultant

HOW MUCH MONEY DO YOU
WANT TO LEAVE ON THE TABLE?

Imagine finding out ten years into your retirement that you made a mistake when you claimed your Social Security benefits—a mistake that resulted in your leaving more than $250,000 on the table. How might losing out on that amount of money affect your retirement? Will you be forced to downgrade your lifestyle or spend money you had planned to leave for your kids? Will you run out of money? And what could you have done differently to have a better outcome?

This might sound like a worst-case scenario, but the reality is that thousands of Americans make this mistake every year. Many of them could have prevented such loss with a little awareness and planning. That's why we set about to write this book: To make you aware of how Social Security can interact with your other assets, and how to potentially uncover thousands of dollars in additional benefits.

WHAT'S AT STAKE?

The unfortunate reality is that Social Security is a one-time decision that many people get wrong. How wrong depends on the situation, but the monetary magnitude of the mistake can range anywhere from tens of thousands to hundreds of thousands of dollars.

Take the situation of a typical couple, Jack and Jane. They are both retiring this year at age 62. To maintain their lifestyle in retirement, they will need $65,000 a year in after-tax income adjusted annually for inflation. They have saved about $600,000 in IRAs (Individual Retirement Accounts) but have no additional savings accounts or other assets besides their home. They have literally hundreds of options at their disposal for electing to take their Social Security benefits, but in this example, we'll examine two possible scenarios.

ANNUAL INCOME AND YEARS IN RETIREMENT

In scenario 1, Jack and Jane both elect to start claiming benefits early at age 62. In scenario 2, they both follow a planning process in an effort to maximize their family Social Security benefit.

Scenario 1: Both Elect at Age 62

If Jack takes his benefit at age 62, he will get $1,544 per month based on his lifetime earnings record. If Jane takes her benefit at 62, she will get $1,163 per month based on her earnings record. Assuming their IRAs continue to grow at an average of 6% and inflation grows at 4%, Jack and Jane will fully exhaust their IRAs at their age 80, leaving their Social Security to provide them with only 50% of their needed income each month thereafter to live on, as you can see in the graph. This is not ideal. They will be forced to curb their lifestyle and alter their financial plans dramatically.

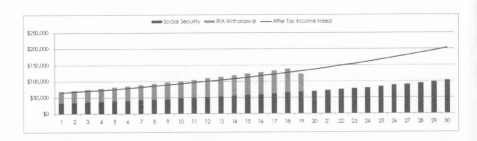

Scenario 2: With Proper Planning

There are many options when it comes to Social Security planning, all of which will be explored in this book, but we wanted to provide you with a quick illustration to demonstrate the power of such planning.

Let's say that rather than electing to take their Social Security benefits early at age 62, Jack and Jane begin spending down their IRAs, which will allow them to *delay* taking their Social Security benefits. Jack then files for benefits when he reaches his full retirement age of 66 and immediately requests what is called a "voluntary suspension" (see chapter 3) of those benefits. Meanwhile, Jane elects to take only her "spousal benefit" (also explained in chapter 3) of approximately $1,204 when she reaches her full retirement age of 66.

Then, when she turns 70, she will switch over to her own benefit, which by then will have grown to approximately $2,800 per month. And when Jack reaches age 70, he then reinstates the benefit he had voluntarily suspended, which by then will have grown to about $3,718. By following this strategy, they will have used up most of their IRA savings, depleting it to about $170,000 by the time they turn 70. But they will also have realized about $61,000 in "spousal benefits" that would otherwise have been lost had they both elected to start collecting Social Security at 62, and they will have increased their own benefits to a total of approximately $78,000 per year.

In all, by spending down their IRAs first rather than claiming their Social Security benefits early, Jack and Jane will have increased their total monthly Social Security benefit by 76%!

Assuming they live to age 90, implementing this strategy may result in realizing $285,000 in additional benefit income for each of them over the exact same life expectancy, from the exact same Social Security system—all because they made Social Security planning a priority in their financial plan, which is shown in the next graphic.

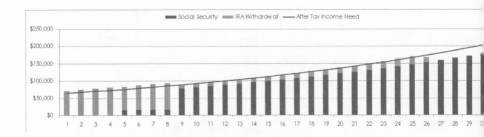

Furthermore, as a result of this planning strategy, their IRAs will now last them until age 87. And even if they spent the entire balance in those IRAs, they would still have almost 88% (rather than 50%) of their required income coming in each month from Social Security.

It's important to note here that Social Security benefits are taxed differently than other income streams, which we will cover later in this book. In this case, total Federal taxes paid over their lifetimes under scenario 1 would total about $147,000, and total taxes paid under scenario 2 would run about $80,000. (Authors' calculations based on 2013 tax brackets projected forward at 4% over a thirty-year time horizon.)

What does this mean for you? In all, a longer portfolio life, a stronger foundation if unforeseen market events negatively impact the portfolio, and a lower tax burden over time mean this couple can sustain a higher lifestyle in retirement as a result of starting their planning with Social Security. With good planning, you may be able to do the same.

"[Social Security] is not intended as a substitute for private savings, pension plans, and insurance protection. It is, rather, intended as the foundation upon which these other forms of protection be soundly built. Thus, the individual's own work, his planning and his thrift will bring him a higher standard of living upon his retirement, or his family a higher standard of living in the event of his death, than would otherwise be the case. Hence the system both encourages thrift and self-reliance, and helps to prevent destitution in our national life."

—President Dwight D. Eisenhower,
January 14, 1954

Why Does Social Security Matter So Much?

The number one concern for retirees is running out of money followed by the ability to afford health care, according to a study conducted by Met Life's Mature Market Institute. When you consider the current environment—with increased life expectancies, disappearing pensions, an economy in turmoil, interest rates at historic lows, and the possibility of higher inflation and income tax hikes in the future—the fear of running out of money is completely justified.

The financial risks in retirement may be completely different from the risks you face during your working years. While working, you have time on your side—more time to save and more time to recover from mistakes. During retirement, more time equals higher inflation, more expenses, and a greater likelihood of running out of money. Unfortunately, Social Security does not immediately come to most people's minds as a solution to this problem.

First, we've been conditioned to believe that we will get short-changed if we wait too long to start claiming benefits. The conventional wisdom (or fear) among retirees is that if they delay Social Security benefits, they will either die before they can get their money's worth or the system itself will go broke.

Although dying early is a risk, it is a risk that can be defined and mitigated. We know exactly how much of our own money we will need to spend in order to delay benefits. So dying early is a limited risk from a financial perspective.

A much greater risk than dying early is living too long. Over the course of a twenty-five or thirty-year retirement, inflation and taxes can erode the purchasing power of all our assets and possibly deplete them well before we die. We all know someone who lived to be 95 or even 100. We don't know what inflation will look like in the future or what the performance of our other investments will be over a long period of time. That's why longevity is a much greater risk to a successful retirement.

If You're Over 55, You're Safe. Relatively.

As for the Social Security program itself, when you actually dig into the solvency of the system, you will see that *Social Security is one of the best-funded programs in the country*—and that relatively minor changes may be needed to ensure the system remains solvent *indefinitely*. Furthermore, none of the proposed changes should significantly impact anybody who is currently over the age of 55.

Second, Social Security is often ignored because the financial services industry often talks about the importance of saving and investing. Why? Because the industry has a vested interest in clients' ignoring their Social Security options.

If you simply elect upon retirement to take your benefits, your financial advisors will have more of your money under management with them, at least in the short term. More assets under management means more fees or commissions for them.

This is not to say that there is anything wrong with saving money, only that saving is just one part of the retirement planning solution. The other part of the equation is to make every effort to maximize the assets you already have—*including Social Security*.

An Asset, Not Just a Benefit

Most Americans' perceptions of Social Security are flawed. Chances are, the first time you've heard Social Security referred to as an *asset* is in this book.

Most people think of Social Security as "money from the government." But it is not just a government giveaway. Social Security is social *insurance*. We all pay in and we have a measure of control over how our benefit is paid out. Therefore, we all have a responsibility to ourselves and to our families to make sure this asset is maximized to the fullest extent possible.

Social Security is completely unique as a retirement asset.

- It is adjusted annually for inflation, which means that as the price of goods and services goes up, so does your Social Security check.
- It is tax-advantaged. In other words, at worst, only 85 cents of every Social Security dollar is treated as taxable income, and for most middle-income people, there are terrific opportunities to lessen that even further, as will be explained in chapter 5.
- It will pay you for as long as you are alive (even if you live to 100 or beyond). We hope you live to collect Social Security for a long time.
- It is backed by a government promise. The concern should not be for government "default" on Social Security obligations.

No other asset that you could buy in the private sector possesses all four of these characteristics. Even financial products designed for retirement, such as annuities, are expensive to purchase when compared to additional Social Security benefits, especially in the current interest rate environment (because interest rates are so low).

Because Social Security may account for a large portion of your retirement income, because a bad election decision can cost you thousands of dollars, and because it offers unique benefits unmatched by any other asset, Social Security should be *the foundation* of a well-thought-out retirement plan.

That's why you should work with a financial advisor who understands Social Security and has the tools and knowledge to make it the foundation of your retirement plan by helping you determine first what your expenses will be in retirement. This step is extremely important because if you know how much you plan on spending in retirement, you will know how much income your assets need to generate.

Next, you need to look at how you can maximize your fixed retirement income sources such as pensions and immediate annuities. As we noted earlier, longevity is your main concern in retirement and fixed/inflation-adjusted income sources (such as Social Security) are your best defense.

With regard to maximizing Social Security, the techniques we talk about in this book are not about how to get the highest payment for yourself today. Not at all. We are focused on how to get the greatest benefit for you and your spouse over your entire lifetime.

Usually that means delaying at least a portion of your benefits and using creative election strategies. Once you've determined when and how to take Social Security, you can decide which assets you'll use to fill the income gap until you do start taking benefits. You'll know how much growth you'll need to achieve with your other assets and therefore how much risk they must be exposed to in order to achieve that growth. Finally, you or your advisor can design your investment strategy around those assumptions.

How to Use This Book

This book will show you how through proper planning you may achieve the most from Social Security—income that would allow other assets in your portfolio, such as your IRA, to remain in a more conservative, less risky investment position and your overall retirement to be more secure.

The following descriptions of each chapter will take you through the often-confusing landscape of claiming the most Social Security benefits. Much of this information is not readily available even from the Social Security Administration, which is not set up to respond to many of the types of questions that proper Social Security planning raises.

In our opinion, each of these chapters is a must-read for anyone who is serious about proper retirement planning. So be sure to read these descriptions to get a leg up on what's being covered in each chapter:

- **Chapter 1:** *Not an Entitlement—Let's Call It Social Insurance* shows how Social Security is a critical part of your overall retirement plan and can be a more effective tool than even private insurance in helping to protect you against the financial risks of your retirement years.

- **Chapter 2:** *Benefits Basics: Surprising Ways Social Security Works (Stuff You Need to Know Now)* explains the fundamentals of claiming Social Security benefits, from how benefits are calculated to choosing when and how to take them. These are the basics you must know in order to make some of the key decisions of your lifetime.

- **Chapter 3:** *Beyond the Basics: How Social Security Really Works (So Make It Work for You)* explores the more unusual Social Security claiming tools and strategies available to you, ranging from restricting your application to spousal or survivor benefits to the "file and suspend" strategy to accruing Delayed Retirement Credits and the specific issues facing government employees. You'll learn about Switch Strategies®—how to file for a limited benefit for a period of time, then later switch to a larger benefit.

- **Chapter 4:** *Making Income Last in Retirement (or How to Spend All Your Kids' Inheritance)* shows how to calculate your living costs in retirement and how to better utilize your Social Security benefits by viewing them as a key ingredient in your asset allocation mix. And why not spend your children's inheritance?

- **Chapter 5:** *Keeping a Sharp Eye on Taxes (Do You Really Want to Pay More Than You Need To?)* shows how to navigate the often-muddy waters of paying tax on your retirement income, including Social Security, and provides strategies for keeping your tax bill low.

- **Chapter 6:** *Get It Right the First Time* looks at your options if you've already made a Social Security claim. Are there "do-overs" once you've made this important and often irrevocable decision? Maybe.

- **Resources:** We also include a list of resources for additional information on Social Security, including important Social Security Administration publications, and My Living Expenses Worksheet.

QUESTIONS TO ASK FINANCIAL ADVISORS (AND THE ANSWERS YOU SHOULD EXPECT TO HEAR)

To accomplish your retirement objectives you can't afford to choose just any financial advisor from the Yellow Pages or your brother-in-law or neighbor's cousin. You will need someone who is up to date on the role Social Security can play in preserving the purchasing power of *all* your assets for years to come. You need to find someone who can help you realize your retirement dream.

Not every financial advisor is equipped to help with Social Security. Be sure to check out potential advisors to make sure they have actual expertise. Here are a few questions and the answers you should expect to hear:

You ask: "I'm looking for lifetime, guaranteed, inflation-protected income. Where should I start?"

Red Flag: If potential advisors say anything other than Social Security (for example, if they immediately suggest an annuity), they may not be right for you. Substantial research indicates that "buying" more Social Security income is much more efficient than buying more annuity income.

You ask: "How can I get the most out of Social Security?"

Red Flag: Be worried if you hear this: "You have plenty of other assets. Social Security won't be that important to you." The average couple receives $556,000 in lifetime Social Security benefits, according to the Urban Institute. You would have to have *a lot* of money not to care about a half million dollars.

You ask: "How will my Social Security income be taxed?"

Red Flag: "It's 85% taxable." Potentially correct, but it doesn't have to be—especially if income is less than $100,000. Look for someone who can help you understand your tax issues.

You ask: "How do we get more from our spousal/survivor benefits?"

Red Flag: If they don't know about Switch Strategies, such as restricted application and file and suspend, which allow you to collect spousal benefits while allowing your own benefit to continue growing, keep looking.

You ask: "Since Social Security is broke, shouldn't I just take it as early as possible?"

Red Flag: If they stumble here, this tells you they're not really doing Social Security planning regularly because they would be getting this question all the time. If they agree with you, they're probably a salesperson. They probably will want you to take Social Security income and invest it with them. The difference between a salesperson and an advisor is that a salesperson will let you go down the wrong path if it results in a sale—an advisor won't.

NOT AN ENTITLEMENT–
LET'S CALL IT SOCIAL INSURANCE

What *Is* Social Security?

Ask any young widow with children what Social Security means to her and she will very likely mention little or nothing about retirement. What she will tell you about is how Social Security is enabling her to keep food on the table, as she and her children are receiving benefits under her deceased husband's record, making the benefits she and her family are receiving the equivalent of life insurance protection.

Ask any severely disabled person what Social Security means to him and he'll very likely tell you a story that also has nothing to do with retirement but everything to do with the ability to survive in the absence of the capacity to work.

What each is saying can be summed up this way: Social Security is so much more than a retirement benefit. Many feel it is a safety net, a system of social insurance that protects all workers and their families against the risk of the "Big Bads." These risks change as we grow older and the focus of Social Security changes along with these risks to help protect people.

The "Big Bads"

Markets don't cooperate.

Financial advisors are fond of quoting Jeremy Siegel, the famous Wharton School of Economics professor and author of *Stocks for the Long Run: The Definitive Guide to Financial Market Returns & Long Term Investment Strategies,* who has analyzed 200 years of market data in an effort to demonstrate that stocks over long periods of time outperform all other asset classes.

Although the data are powerful and may provide a strong argument for equity investment, many conclusions drawn by Siegel and his followers miss an important point: nobody lives 200 years in retirement. Over any five- or ten-year stretch, there can be a terrific or awful run in the market. It takes only one awful run at the wrong time, or a mediocre run for an extended period, to decimate a retirement portfolio. Maybe even yours.

Investing in solid companies can make all the sense in the world, but not in the absence of drawing a clear picture of how much money you need to have to survive. Social Security is one key backdrop that isn't impacted by market performance.

Extreme longevity.

As most people can't know how long they'll live, they don't consider this factor when saving for retirement. According to one analysis conducted in 2008 by the auditing firm Ernst & Young, an estimated nine out of ten middle-income ($75,000 per annum) newly retired couples who don't have pension income outside of Social Security are at risk of outliving their savings, which could force them to eventually reduce their standard of living, on average, by 38%.

When the study was updated in 2009, the number at risk in that same class rose to nineteen out of twenty, and the projected reduction in standard of living rose to 41%. If you were used to making $75,000 a year and your lifestyle was built around that level of income, how much change does a 41% reduction represent? How much of your current lifestyle could you enjoy if you only had $45,000 rather than $75,000 coming in the door each year?

Inflation.

Retirees who rely on fixed income are especially vulnerable to rises in the cost of goods and services, otherwise known as inflation. In the 1970s, inflation averaged 7.06% annually. That means a lifestyle that would have cost you $50,000 in 1970 would cost you almost $100,000 just ten years later.

At the same time, the stock market, as measured by the S&P 500, had a compounded annual return of 5.8%. The combination of these factors meant that a portfolio may have actually lost value to inflation through the 1970s. In short, during periods of high inflation, equity investments historically have not kept pace.

Even in the absence of inflationary shocks like we saw in the 1970s and early 1980s, the long-term average inflation rate in the United States has been about 3.75%. If you only experience average inflation, it would take twenty years for your required income to double in order for you to be able to keep the same standard of living you have today.

In short, Social Security benefits may offer strong protection against inflation because they are designed to increase each year in order to keep up with inflation. The graph shows the historical Cost of Living Adjustments (COLAs) applied to Social Security benefits. Note the particular adjustments during the high-inflation periods of the 1970s through 1980s.

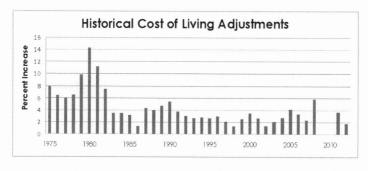

Percentage of Change Each Year in Cost of Living Adjustments Applied to Social Security Benefits (Source: Social Security Administration, www.ssa.gov/oact/cola/colaseries.html)

Social Security Covers Your Risk

Social Security is unique in that it protects against all three main retirement risks: inflation, market (sequence risk), and longevity (how long you live). (Just to clarify, market risk is the risk your investments will not perform as they are needed to meet your goals. Sequence risk assumes the average performance will be okay for you, but the dips will occur at the wrong time, such as in the first five years of your retirement.) Social Security is adjusted annually for inflation, it's tax-advantaged, it will pay as long as you live, and it's backed by a government promise.

It's All About Risk Management

Social Security is one of the most effective ways to protect yourself against these and other "Big Bads." Under a typical insurance company plan, you as the buyer of the policy agree to pay premiums to the company in exchange for a guarantee that it will pay you benefits after a predefined event occurs and you put in a claim. The underlying principle of social insurance is similar: you contribute now for the intent that you will receive protection later. Social Security is protection offered by the government, not by a company, against risks to a broad group of its citizens.

Social insurance is different than private insurance in that it is not a for-profit business, thus social insurance programs have a focus on adequacy, and near-universality of coverage, where private insurance has a focus on profitability.

Social Insurance Benefits
Date Back to the Civil War

"Although Social Security was not created until 1935, the U.S. did have an important and far earlier precursor in the form of the Civil War Pension Program. Implemented shortly after the start of the war, that program initially provided benefits for soldiers disabled in combat, as well as to war widows and orphans. The program was later expanded to include all non–war-related disabilities, as well as old-age pension benefits to soldiers and their families. It eventually grew to cover nearly 90% of Civil War veterans and their families.

"The Civil War Pension Program provided an important model for the later development of Social Security with the introduction of family income protection. This model provides replacement of wages not just for workers, but also for their spouses and children in the event of worker disability or death," according to "A Young Person's Guide to Social Security" published by The Economic Policy Institute, 2011.

According to the National Academy of Social Insurance (www.nasi.org),

> Families once bore the primary responsibility for caring for their individual members in bad times,

but modern industrial society has scattered family members to different jobs in different locations. Certain risks we have agreed to confront as a society, rather than as individuals. Citizens have decided, through the political system, that we need financial protection against some of life's difficulties that are hard to face as individuals. These include old age, ill health, unemployment, disability that makes it impossible to work, injury on the job, and the death of a family bread winner. For all these conditions, we rely on help from social insurance programs, which are financed by workers and employers.

An Essential Source of Income

Some politicians and pundits in our society criticize Social Security as an "entitlement program" and have described it from inception as a Ponzi [1] scheme or even as welfare. Since we pay into Social Security for certain benefits, we are, therefore, entitled to claim these benefits when we become eligible. That arrangement certainly doesn't qualify as a Ponzi scheme or as welfare. But does it constitute an "entitlement program"? Let's see.

In America, if you want to drive a car or truck, you are legally required—mandated—to buy auto insurance (liability coverage, at a minimum). And if you have an accident in your car or truck, you are able to put in a benefit claim because of the premiums you've paid. Does that make auto insurance an entitlement program? Only in the sense that you are "entitled" to the benefit you receive because you paid for it.

Likewise when you buy a home, your bank or other mortgager requires—mandates—that you buy homeowner's insurance to protect its investment until the house is paid off. If your house catches fire and you collect benefits on that insurance policy for the damage, does that make homeowner's insurance an entitlement program, or "something-for-nothing" scheme? No. Again, you paid for those benefits you received.

Social Security is social insurance for one of your most basic needs: income. So when you enter the workforce, you are legally required—yes, mandated—to enroll in a system of social insurance for your income by buying into the Social Security program for benefits you will be entitled to when eligible to collect them because you paid for them.

These benefits are designed to replace a percentage of your earnings when you retire, become disabled, or die. What you pay into the system toward those benefits is based on how much you earned during your working life. Higher lifetime earnings result in higher benefits. If there were some years when you did not work or had low earnings, your benefit amount might be lower than if you had worked steadily.

Just How Much of Your Income Will Be Represented by Social Security?

Despite the modest size of monthly benefits, Social Security forms a substantial share of retirement income for most recipients. According to statistics, for the poorest in our country, it is the vast majority of income (88.5%), while for the richest it is still about a fifth (17.1%). For the middle class, over three-fourths (77.3%) of their retirement income comes from Social Security. And even for the upper middle class, Social Security is nearly half (47.8%) of income, according to the EBRI Databook on Employee Benefits.

Social Security is often an essential source of income to its beneficiaries. Although the benefits may seem modest, a study conducted by Eugene Steurle of the Urban Institute shows that a couple with an average wage of $43,500 a year in 2011 who elect to claim benefits at age 65 would receive a lifetime retirement benefit worth $471,000. When viewed this way, Social Security is a valuable asset for just about anyone.

Disability and Survivor Insurance

As we noted earlier, Social Security is more than just benefits for retirees. The life and disability benefits of the system also play a crucial part in providing economic security for many Americans.

In spite of all the advances we've seen in medicine, the risk of disability and premature death is still with us. In fact, a 20-year-old worker has a three in ten chance of becoming disabled before reaching retirement age. Social Security offers some protection in this situation. It is one of the most important sources of income for disabled workers and their families.[2]

The value provided to survivors through Social Security is over $476,000, and the value of disability protection for a young disabled worker with a spouse and two children is over $465,000. [3]

When Are You Fully Insured?

To receive a retirement benefit from Social Security based on your own earnings, you must earn a minimum of 40 "credits" (explained later) throughout your working life. You earn these credits through the payroll taxes you pay on your wages.

If you stop working before you have enough credits to qualify for benefits, they will remain on your Social Security record. If you go back to work later on, you can add more credits so that you do qualify. No Social Security retirement benefits can be paid until you have earned the requisite number of credits.

You receive one credit by earning a specified amount of money, for one credit up to four credits a year. For example, in 2013, workers received one credit for every $1,160 earned. So if you earned at least $4,640 in 2013 (4 x $1,160), you would have earned the maximum number of credits for that year.

Starting in 1978, credits received by workers were determined on an annual basis instead of each quarter. The chart shows wages needed to earn one credit for each year from 1978 to 2013.

Year	Earnings	Year	Earnings	Year	Earnings
1978	$250	1993	$590	2008	$1,050
1979	$260	1994	$620	2009	$1,090
1980	$290	1995	$630	2010	$1,120
1981	$310	1996	$640	2011	$1,120
1982	$340	1997	$670	2012	$1,130
1983	$370	1998	$700	2013	$1,160
1984	$390	1999	$740		
1985	$410	2000	$780		
1986	$440	2001	$830		
1987	$460	2002	$870		
1988	$470	2003	$890		
1989	$500	2004	$900		
1990	$520	2005	$920		
1991	$540	2006	$970		
1992	$570	2007	$1,000		

Wages Needed to Earn One Credit for Each Year from 1978 to 2013

You can earn up to four credits per year, so if you, for example, earned $4,640 in 2013, even if you earned all of it in January, you would receive all four credits for the year. In other words, it takes ten years of work at very modest levels of earnings to qualify for Social Security retirement benefits.

> "We can never insure one-hundred percent of the population against one-hundred percent of the hazards and vicissitudes of life. But we have tried to frame a law which will give some measure of protection to the average citizen and to his family against the loss of a job and against poverty-ridden old age. This law, too, represents a cornerstone in a structure which is being built, but is by no means complete. ... It is, in short, ... a law that will take care of human needs and at the same time provide for the United States an economic structure of vastly greater soundness."
>
> — President Franklin D. Roosevelt,
> August 14, 1935

SEIZE THE OPPORTUNITY

Despite its importance, today's retirees and pre-retirees know surprisingly little about the mechanics of Social Security and how they can maximize their benefit. Retirees are unsure where to turn for advice when making this complex decision.

Consider these statistics, gathered from a 2011 survey called "Social Security Planning: A Cornerstone of Your Financial Practice" from Social Security Timing. It was a survey of 532 married people between the ages of 60 and 66 conducted by one of the authors:

- Only 27% of people are aware of the ability to file a restricted application or voluntarily suspend benefits.
- Some 77% of people think they can go to the Social Security office for advice, when in fact Social Security Administration personnel are not trained or equipped to dispense anything more than monthly benefit amounts at different election ages. Furthermore, the Social Security Administration actually prohibits its representatives from dispensing advice.
- Of all respondents, 57% said they would expect their financial planner to help them analyze their options and make the right decision.
- The same percentage of people said they would actually look for a new advisor if their current one couldn't help them with Social Security.

In short, the vast majority of today's retirees and pre-retirees don't know that Social Security planning strategies exist and often don't know where to turn for the complex analysis required to make the right decision.

That's where this book comes in. With uncertainty in the economy and fears of outliving their money, many people are hungry for advice on how to maximize their Social Security. They're unsure of where to turn, but they're beginning to look to us in the financial industry for help.

Retire a Winner Checklist

We have presented summary questions for you to consider at the end of each chapter. These checklists throughout the book should help you to determine whether this is a do-it-yourself endeavor or whether you need an advisor with this expertise. Remember, Uncle Sam offers no "do-overs." It's really up to you whether you retire a winner.

Have you addressed the following issues?

☐ I understand the Social Security Administration and its employees are neither authorized nor equipped to provide me with the details I will need to make the proper election decision for achieving my *overall retirement income goals.*

☐ Since I have paid into the Social Security system when I began working and my various employers had to make dollar-for-dollar matches to my account, I consider Social Security to be a significant asset in my portfolio and expect my advisor to view it that way also.

☐ I will be wary of financial advisors who urge me to start taking Social Security benefits early in order to retain more of my money under their management.

☐ I understand the risk management role of Social Security in my retirement income portfolio and have proactively considered the impact of market and investment risk, the risk of living a very long life, and the risk of inflation.

BENEFITS BASICS: SURPRISING WAYS SOCIAL SECURITY WORKS (STUFF YOU NEED TO KNOW NOW)

CALCULATING BENEFITS—THE KEY MOVING PARTS

C hoosing when to take Social Security benefits can be one of the most important decisions you will make in your lifetime. It can make the difference between whether your retirement plan will see to it that your money is likely to outlive you—or the other way around.

In order to decide when to claim, it's important for you to understand a bit about the process of how benefits are calculated by the Social Security Administration—a formula that consists of the following key moving parts, all of them specific to you:

- Average Indexed Monthly Earnings (AIME)
- Primary Insurance Amount (PIA)
- Full Retirement Age
- Delayed Retirement Credits
- The Longevity Factor

In this chapter, we'll discuss each of these in order.

Key Moving Part #1:
Average Indexed Monthly Earnings (AIME)

Social Security retirement benefits are based on your record of earnings that are subject to Social Security tax over your highest thirty-five years of Social Security–covered work. Before comparing all of your years of earnings, Social Security creates a table of values that are multiplied by your past earnings to put them on an equal footing with earnings in the year you turn age 60 (see the following figure for an example using an individual who is earning the Social Security average wage of $41,334.97 in 2011 dollars, as defined within the calculator, and turning 62 years of age in 2012). These numbers were calculated using ANYPIA (Social Security's detailed calculator available at www.ssa.gov).

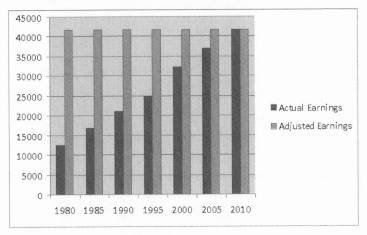

Actual Earnings vs. Adjusted Earnings

Any earnings you have after age 60, which is called your "base year," are not indexed. Once Social Security has adjusted *all* your past earnings in this manner, it will then identify the highest thirty-five years, average them, and divide the average by twelve (the number of months in each year) to come up with what is called your AIME or Average Indexed Monthly Earnings—the first step in the benefit calculation process.

If you have fewer than thirty-five years of earnings, the years that you don't have earnings still count in the formula, but they count as zeroes. An extra year of work can have a substantial impact on your AIME and translate into higher benefits.

Get a copy of your Social Security statement by visiting www.ssa. gov and clicking on "My Social Security." Answer a few short questions to set up an account, and you can access your statement online. Review this statement to be sure all of your earnings have been recorded.

Occasionally we will see a client who is missing years of earnings. Either the earnings weren't reported to Social Security or they were reported under an incorrect Social Security number. Regardless of the reason, if you are missing years of earnings, you will want to get them corrected, because you could be missing out on benefits.

Key Moving Part #2: Primary Insurance Amount (PIA)

Your Primary Insurance Amount, or PIA, is by definition the amount you will receive if you elect to begin receiving retirement benefits at full retirement age 66. At this age, the benefit is neither reduced for early retirement nor increased for delayed retirement.

The PIA is the sum of three separate percentages of portions, called "bend points" of your AIME. The bend points in the formula change every year based on changes to the national average wage, so you will want to be sure you or your advisor use the appropriate bend points for the year that you initially become eligible to claim benefits. For example, for an individual who first becomes eligible for old-age insurance benefits or disability insurance benefits in 2013, or who dies in 2012 before becoming eligible for benefits, his PIA will be the sum of the following:

- 90% of the first $791 of his AIME, plus
- 32% of his AIME over $791 and through $4,768, plus
- 15% of his AIME over $4,768

Here's an example: Jack Doe's AIME was $5,000. That means, on average over his highest thirty-five years of earnings, he made about $60,000 per year in today's dollars. Therefore, his PIA would be $2,019.34, as shown in this chart (authors' calculation; note: the PIA is then rounded to the next lower dime, so in this case, Jack's PIA would be $2,019.30).

90% of first $791	791 x .9	$711.90
32% of amount between $791 and $4,768	3977 x .32	$1,272.64
15% of the amount over $4,768	232 x .15	$34.80
Total PIA		$2,019.34

How to Calculate PIA

The "bend points" change each year based on changes to the National Average Wage Index, so be sure you are using the right set of bend points when calculating your benefit.

Although somewhat complicated and abstract, the PIA is the basic building block of all benefits, so it must be fully understood by your financial advisor (who should be able to explain it to you). The coordination of spousal benefits, to which we will pay significant attention in chapter 3, depends on the relative PIAs of each spouse, as do survivor benefits paid to surviving spouses or surviving divorced spouses.

In short, if you want to understand how to get the most from Social Security, PIA is a critically important concept.

And You Thought You Wanted to Retire!

If you've had low earnings and/or fewer than thirty-five years of earnings, one additional year of work can have a substantial impact on your AIME, which translates into higher benefits.

Each year, your earnings will be compared to the lowest year of your top thirty-five. If the new earnings amount is higher, it will go into the AIME calculation and result in a bigger benefit. If the new earnings are not higher than any of your top thirty-five, it will *not* go into the AIME calculation, so it also will not cause your benefits to be reduced (unlike the formulas for many private-sector pensions that look to your average salary near the end of your career in determining your monthly payout).

If you have ten years of earnings averaging $25,000 per year, for example, you would have an AIME of $595, of which the entire amount is replaced at 90%, for a full retirement age benefit of $535 per month. One additional year of work at $25,000 would raise your AIME to $654, again replaced at 90% for a benefit amount of $588. So that one additional year of work will have resulted in a 10% increase in your full retirement age benefit for life!

Calculate this now if you're in your late 50s or early 60s. You might decide to work an additional year just for this very reason.

Key Moving Part #3: Full Retirement Age

Your Full Retirement Age is an important consideration in the decision of when to claim benefits to achieve maximum advantage because, as we've noted earlier in this chapter, taking benefits prior to full retirement age causes your monthly benefit amount to be reduced, and taking benefits after full retirement age causes your monthly benefit amount to be increased. The latter also gives you some other options that we will discuss later in this chapter.

Full retirement age is 66 for people born between 1943 and 1954, and gradually increases to age 67 for those born in 1960 or thereafter. Check the chart for your year of birth and you can see the specifics of your full retirement age, depending on the year you were born.

Year of Birth	Full Retirement Age
1943–1954	66
1955	66 and 2 months
1956	66 and 4 months
1957	66 and 6 months
1958	66 and 8 months
1959	66 and 10 months
1960 or later	67

When Will You Reach Full Retirement Age?

In theory, if you elect to take benefits prior to your full retirement age, you will get a smaller benefit for a longer period of time. If you elect after your full retirement age, you will get a larger benefit for a shorter period of time.

For single people, the decision of whether to elect early or later can be as simple as answering the question: Do I think I'll live long enough to make waiting worth it? For example, if you decide to elect at 66, how long will it take for the larger payments to make up for the payments you missed from ages 62 to 65? This is called the "break-even" point (see where the lines intersect on the graph?), and it is the yardstick most often used by people in looking at whether to elect early or late. But for married couples, widows, and widowers, and people who are divorced, the decision is much more complex, as you will see in chapter 3.

Break Even Chart

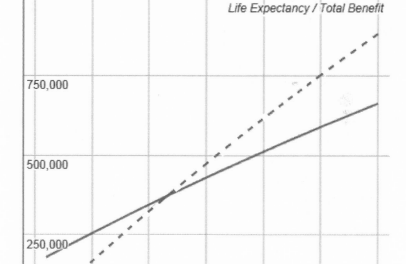

When Will You Reach the Break-Even Point by Electing Benefits at Age 66?

This figure assumes 1% Real Discount Rate, $2,500 Primary Insurance Amount. The dotted line shows cumulative retirement benefits if claimed at age 62 and 1 month. The solid line portrays cumulative benefits if claimed at age 70. The break-even point is about age 82. (Source: www.socialsecuritytiming.com)

Three Factors: You Can Control One of Them

How much you receive from Social Security depends on your earnings record, when you elect to start taking benefits, and how long you expect to live. Since you can't go back and change your earnings record, and you have minimal control over how long you live, calculating an expected lifetime benefit is largely affected by when you elect to receive benefits.

Key Moving Part #4: Delayed Retirement Credits

As you've already learned, if you decide to retire early, your retirement benefit will be lower than if you wait until later to take it. Social Security describes the benefit amount you receive at full retirement age as your PIA, which is another way of saying "full retirement age benefit."

Here's how things work: If you elect to claim benefits as soon as you are eligible (at age 62), your benefits will be reduced 5/9th of 1% for each month up to 36 months, then 5/12th of 1% for each month over 36 months. For example, if your full retirement age was 66, but you decided to claim at 62, you would be claiming 48 months early, thus your reduction would be 5/9 x 36 + 5/12 x 12 for a total reduction of 25%. [Note that widows and widowers can begin receiving Social Security benefits at age 60, or at age 50 if they are disabled. For more on this, see chapter 3.]

If you're a Baby Boomer, claiming at 62 would therefore result in a 25% *permanent* reduction in your monthly benefit amount than if you had waited until your full retirement age to start claiming. Excluding any Cost of Living Adjustments (COLAs) that may be added to your benefit subsequently, this means you would receive that reduced benefit for the remaining years you collect Social Security.

On the other hand, claiming after your full retirement age has the opposite effect: It *increases* your benefits. This is because of what are called "Delayed Retirement Credits." Each additional year you delay your benefit election past full retirement age gets you an automatic 8% increase in your monthly benefit amount.

To get an idea of what the effect on your financial picture might be if you claimed your Social Security benefits early or if you delayed electing until age 66 or beyond, see the next two graphics. The key point to understand here is that the dollar difference between claiming early and claiming later grows over time due to compounding Cost of Living Adjustments (COLAs). The average cost of living since automatic Cost of Living Adjustments went into effect in 1974 through 2011 has been 4.16% (authors' calculation based on COLA Data Series at www.ssa.gov).

The gap between taking early and late grows because of compounding COLAs. Your Social Security statements do not include COLAs, so factor that in before making a decision.

You and your financial advisor must look deeper into when to start claiming Social Security benefits—and at Social Security in general as an important asset in your planning—in order to try to achieve maximum results and help alleviate your retirement fears of running out of money.

Key Moving Part #5: The Longevity Factor

Today living another thirty years in retirement is a lot more common than it was in 1980, and some people today may even live forty years in retirement. Likewise, the rules formulating the various benefit amounts people received in 1980 have changed over the years.

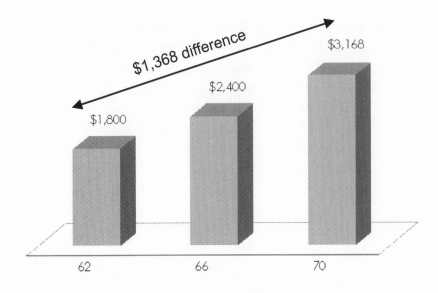

Sample Monthly Benefits Without COLAs

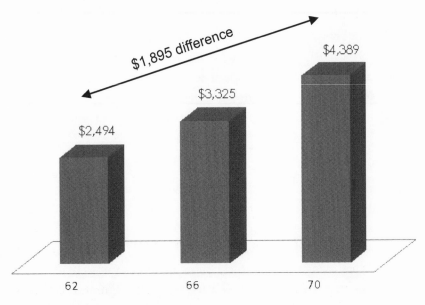

Sample Monthly Benefits at Age 70
(with an assumed annual COLA of 4.16%)

These changes have created even more of an incentive for people today to consider delaying the taking of their benefits to a later date.

For example, let's look at a fellow who was making $20,000 per year prior to his retirement in 1980. Back then the average wage in the United States was $12,513 a year. For Social Security purposes, earnings were taxed only up to $25,900. Today the average annual wage in the U.S. is $41,673, and earnings are taxed up $110,100 for Social Security.

So in 1980, making $20,000 a year afforded this individual a very comfortable upper-middle-income lifestyle. He was not a "maximum earner," but he was an above-average or "high earner" as far as his Social Security or Federal Insurance Contributions Act (FICA) contribution was concerned. He likely retired with a pension from his employer too, which was also a lot more common back then.

> "Social Security ... is not a dole or a device for giving everybody something for nothing. True Social Security must consist of rights which are earned rights—guaranteed by the law of the land."
>
> —President Harry Truman,
> August 13, 1945

For purposes of this example, let's say he took his pension in a lump sum in order to be able to control the amount of his withdrawals. If he took his Social Security benefit when it first became available at age 62, his benefit would have been $395 a month. Between 1980 and today, Cost of Living Adjustments (COLAs) would have raised that amount to around $1,083 a month. If he wanted to maintain the same purchasing power, he would have had to increase withdrawals from his pension as well. A $1,000 per month withdrawal then would need to be $2,740 per month now.

Furthermore, in 1980, full retirement age was age 65, so taking benefits early at 62 cost him less of a reduction in benefits; he received about 80% of what he would have gotten had he waited until reaching full retirement age. There was also a much smaller increase from the accruing of Delayed Retirement Credits than now. If he delayed until age 70, he would only get 1.15 times what he would have gotten at age 65. So, for him, delaying likely didn't make sense.

Someone who takes benefits at age 62 today would get only 75% of what he would have gotten at full retirement age, which is now 66, and if he elected even later at age 70, he would get an increase 1.32 times greater than at age 66. A retiree in 1980 would only increase his monthly benefits by 43% by delaying from age 62 to age 70. A retiree in 2013 can increase his benefits by 76% by delaying the same amount of time (authors' calculations using www.ssa.gov ANYPIA software).

What this all boils down to is that the decision of *when* to start taking your Social Security benefits is more critical for today's retirees than it was for their parents' generation. The income difference between a good choice and a poor one is much more substantial, and since life expectancies are longer, the total lifetime difference between a good decision and a poor one is even greater.

What If You Continue to Work?

Here's another reason why just looking at "what you get when" in making an election decision is an insufficient strategy. You can choose to claim Social Security early, yet continue to work and still receive benefits. However, your benefits will be reduced if your earnings exceed certain limits before reaching your full retirement age.

For example, if your full retirement age is 66 and you start claiming benefits early at age 62 but continue to work either full- or part-time, $1 in benefits will be deducted for each $2 in earnings you have above the annual limit. (In 2013 that limit was $15,120.)

In the year when you reach full retirement age, your benefits will be reduced $1 for every $3 you earn over a different annual limit ($40,080 in 2013, until the month when you actually turn your full retirement age). After that you can keep working and your Social Security benefit will not be reduced no matter how much you earn.

Retire a Winner Checklist

Have you addressed the following issues?

☐ I have looked at more than a "break-even" analysis in considering the best age for me to start claiming Social Security benefits.

☐ I have calculated not just the delayed credits I can accrue, but have also considered the potential COLAs for all deferral years past age 62 in considering my election strategy.

☐ I have relied on unbiased information in forming an opinion on the long-term viability of my Social Security maximization and retirement income plan.

☐ I have considered my life expectancy before electing how to claim my Social Security benefits.

BEYOND THE BASICS:
HOW SOCIAL SECURITY REALLY WORKS
(SO MAKE IT WORK FOR YOU)

S o far in this book, our main topic of conversation has centered on the rules and considerations surrounding the claiming of Social Security benefits by individuals. In this chapter, we'll delve into the rules and considerations surrounding family claims (that is, spousal and survivor benefits) as well as the wrinkles that apply to government employees. These special rules add considerable complexity, *but also opportunity*, for you to get more from the system.

WHAT ARE SPOUSAL BENEFITS?

Social Security offers three distinct types of benefits for retired workers and/or their spouses:

- Retired Worker Benefit, which is based on that worker's own earnings record
- Spousal Benefit, which provides the worker's spouse with a benefit once the worker has claimed his (or her) own benefit
- Widow or Widower's Benefit (also known as the Survivor Benefit), which provides a surviving spouse with a benefit after a worker's death

To be eligible for the spousal benefit, a spouse must be at least 62, married for at least one year, and the other spouse must have filed for his (or her) retired worker benefit from Social Security.

Let's look at Lynn and Bruce. If eligible, Lynn would be able to receive up to half of her husband Bruce's Primary Insurance Amount (PIA). In other words, the amount of the spousal benefit is determined by when the spouse elects to take the benefit, not when the person under whose record the spouse is claiming the benefit elects to take the benefit.

Who Does Social Security Consider to Be Married?

We're often asked, "Are same-sex marriages recognized by the Social Security Administration for spouse benefits?" Until June 26th, 2013, the answer was no.

On June 26th, a landmark Supreme Court Decision was issued that overturned the Defense of Marriage Act (DOMA) as unconstitutional. As a result of this decision, same-sex couples who are married in states that recognize same-sex marriages will be eligible to collect Social Security benefits under the same set of rules as traditional married couples.

If you file for benefits prior to your full retirement age, you are considered—or *deemed*—by the Social Security Administration to have filed for *all* benefits to which you are entitled. But at full retirement age and beyond (or at any time for widows), there are ways you can modify your or your spouse's Social Security application to *increase* your lifetime benefits.

One way is with what is called a "restricted application," and the other way is to use a "voluntary suspension." These techniques can be combined in several creative ways that we call Switch Strategies®, which involve the election of a limited benefit initially, then a "switch" to a larger benefit later.

For a single family, it is not unusual to be able to receive an additional $20,000 to $50,000 or more in benefits from applying these strategies. In fact, a Boston College study has suggested that not using them currently represents more $10 billion left on the table in unclaimed Social Security benefits. [4]

Who Earns More?

Can a higher-earning spouse receive spousal benefits on the lower-earning spouse's record? Yes, generally speaking the higher earner is able to receive a spousal benefit if at full retirement age or later he or she applies *only* for spousal benefits. The higher-earning spouse would then be entitled to a benefit of half of the lower-earning spouse's PIA.

How Do "Switch Strategies®" Work?

Once you reach your full retirement age, you have the option to restrict your application to exclude retirement benefits. If the retirement benefit is excluded, it will continue to build delayed retirement "credits" of 8% per year if you were born in 1943 or later.

For example, Mike, who was born in 1950 and has earned more than his wife, Sheila, over their respective working lives, and is therefore considered to be the "higher-earning spouse," decides he wants to wait until age 70 to begin collecting his own Social Security. By restricting his application to only spousal benefits available under Sheila's record, he could claim half of her PIA (without reducing her benefit), while still allowing his own benefit to build Delayed Retirement Credits.

At age 70, he would then switch to his own benefit, which would have grown to 132% of his PIA because of those delayed credits. Alternatively, Sheila, the "lower-earning spouse," could restrict her application to only her spousal benefit while continuing to claim delayed credits on her earnings record. The restricted application can be used to help increase lifetime income (as well as survivor's benefits, which we'll discuss later).

What the Social Security Representatives Don't Tell You

When you contact the Social Security office, the individual you meet with or speak to may have been trained to help you identify the highest benefit you can get *today*, not necessarily over your lifetime, and likely not over the joint lives of you and your spouse. As a result, you are unlikely to hear about these techniques from Social Security. But make sure to discuss this with your financial advisors to make sure they are knowledgeable about how these can work for you.

The second technique is the voluntary suspension. Spousal benefits are not available until the higher-earning spouse has filed for his or her own benefits. The Senior Citizens' Freedom to Work Act of 2000 allows a worker to earn Delayed Retirement Credits after filing for benefits if requesting not to receive benefits during a given period. As a result, a higher-earning spouse can file for benefits, then immediately suspend the benefit, and continue to earn delayed credits of 8% annually.

If we continue to use Mike and Sheila as an example of this strategy, Mike (the higher earner) could file and suspend in order to make Sheila (the lower-earning spouse) eligible for spousal benefits under his earnings record.

It is important to note that under Social Security, each technique is available to the higher-earning spouse (the "primary" earner) or to the lower-earning spouse (the "secondary" earner). Also, the techniques can be combined. For example, the higher earner could file and suspend to make a spousal benefit available to the secondary earner, who could then file a restricted application for just spousal benefits. This would allow both spouses to earn Delayed Retirement Credits on their own earnings records while one of them is still able to collect some benefit now.

All totaled, there are nine basic ways that a benefit on your own record can be combined with a spousal benefit and modified by the restricted application option and/or the voluntary suspension to maximize your Social Security. That means, in simplified terms, that there are 729 options that married couples need to evaluate in order to choose the optimum age combination and election strategy for maximum payoff, which is the subject of the next chapter.

> ## Divorced But Not Forgotten
> ## (at Least by Social Security)
>
> Your former spouse can get the spousal benefit on your Social Security record too, provided the marriage lasted at least ten years. To do so, your ex-spouse must be 62 or older and presently unmarried. The amount of spousal benefit he or she gets has no effect on the amount of benefits you (or your current spouse) can get.
>
> Likewise, if you and your ex-spouse have been divorced for at least two years and both of you are at least age 62, he or she can get the spousal benefit on your record even if you are not yet retired.

The spousal benefit is probably one of the most misunderstood pieces of Social Security planning. Many couples are shocked to learn that a lower-earning or non-earning spouse may be entitled to receive half of the higher-earning spouse's full retirement benefits. Most don't have a clue such an option is available, let alone that they could use it to build their retirement income.

Why don't more people know about and understand this option? Because the financial services industry at large has done a rather poor job of explaining this decision. The industry has neglected to consider Social Security a significant enough asset worthy of being incorporated into an overall financial plan.

Understanding that the spousal benefit entitles the lower-earning spouse to half of the higher-earning spouse's full benefit assumes, however, that the person claiming the spousal benefit has reached full retirement age. If the person claiming the spousal benefit is *under* full retirement age, he or she is going to receive a reduction in benefits similar to what the primary earner would get when applying for regular benefits early—although in the case of the spousal benefit, the reduction is greater at each age. For example, if your full retirement age is 66, at 62, the reduction in the spousal benefit is 30%, not 25%.

Here's an example with some dollar amounts: Let's say Jeff is the primary (higher) earner and he will get $2,000 a month in Social Security benefits at full retirement age. Jeff's spouse, Lorraine, who doesn't have enough of an earnings record herself, decides to take the spousal benefit at age 62. If she and Jeff don't understand the spousal benefit calculation properly, they may automatically think she will be getting half of his $2,000 monthly benefit, or $1,000 a month. But that's only if she too is full retirement age, which she isn't, she's 62. Therefore, her spousal benefit will be $700 a month (70% of 50% of Jeff's $2,000 full retirement age monthly benefit equals 35% or $700).

Making Cents of Social Security Family Benefits

Benefits for family members: In addition to a spouse or ex-spouse, children up to age 18 (or 19 if they are full-time students who have not yet graduated from high school) and disabled children, even if they are age 18 or older, are eligible for Social Security benefits.

Each can receive up to one-half of your full benefit. But there is a limit to the amount of money that can be paid to you and your family. It is called the Family Maximum and is calculated using a formula similar to the PIA formula we discussed earlier. The result of that formula means that the total family benefit received is generally capped—usually at 150% to 180% of your own benefit payment, excluding any Delayed Retirement Credits you earn on your own benefit. If the total benefits due your spouse and children are more than this limit, their benefits will be reduced. Your own benefit will not be affected.

For example: John qualifies for a retirement benefit of $2,000 at his full retirement age, and a Family Maximum PIA of $3,000. His wife, Jane, is the same age and doesn't have enough credits to qualify under her own work record. They have a two-year-old adopted daughter, Jessica. John can claim his $2,000 and Jane could claim her $1,000 because her spousal benefit will be half of his PIA.

Normally, his daughter could claim a benefit of 50% of John's benefit as well, but in this case the Family Maximum would limit the total benefit to $3,000. If they tried to claim benefits for their daughter, the claim would become active, but Jane's benefit would be reduced from $1,000 down to $500, and they would begin receiving $500 for Jessica. The gross benefit to the household would still be $3,000.

This could make sense if John and Jane's benefits were taxable and Jessica has no income or assets in her name as this election would cause the benefits that are being paid to Jessica to be tax free. Interestingly, John could file and suspend and delay his benefit until his age 70. If he did, for purposes of the Family Maximum, they would be treated as if John's PIA were being received the entire time. In other words, he would be receiving $0 between his age 66 and 70 for himself, but he would be treated as if he were receiving $2,000, so Jane and Jessica would still each be limited to $500.

When he turns 70, he would begin receiving $2,640, but would be treated as if he were only receiving $2,000, so Jane and Jessica could still only get $500 each.

COORDINATING YOUR OWN BENEFIT
WITH YOUR SPOUSAL BENEFIT

Let's look at another example of claiming your own benefits with your spousal benefits. Lorraine doesn't have an earnings record of her own, which makes her spousal benefit relatively easy to calculate. If she has a benefit due to her own work, but that benefit is not as high as her spouse's benefit, there is an extra layer of calculation necessary to coordinate the two benefits. In Social Security terms, each benefit is "independently reduced"—then the two parts of the benefit are added together.

Let's say that Lorraine has a PIA of $500 based on her own work. If she elects at 62, she would receive 75% of her PIA after the reduction for early claiming. Lorraine's spousal benefit is actually the excess amount over her own benefit. Remember, you don't get half of your spouse's amount plus your own; your spousal benefit "tops up" to an amount that is half your spouse's PIA if taken at full retirement age.

In this example, $500 is the maximum spousal amount, which is then reduced to 70% for early claiming at age 62. The two benefits are added together, and Lorraine will receive $775 as her benefit amount if she were to elect at 62.

This offers a planning opportunity since each benefit is independently reduced. A plan can therefore be created to intentionally avoid eligibility for one spousal benefit so that there is no reduction on that benefit, which can allow a reduced cash flow to start sooner with the retirement benefit.

"The fortieth anniversary of the Social Security Act celebrates an important milestone in responsible public service. I continue to be impressed by the steady responsiveness of the Social Security program to the changing needs of our people."
—President Gerald R. Ford,
August 9, 1975

What Are Survivor's Benefits?

Social Security offers more than basic retirement benefits to retirees and their spouses. The survivor benefit component also can be quite valuable to your overall financial well-being. But because becoming disabled or dying prematurely is not something people like to contemplate or think about, they seldom fully consider it in their planning. Yet the survivor insurance component of Social Security is one of the most important sources of income for widows and widowers.

In effect, survivor coverage through Social Security is a form of insurance many of you reading this book may not even know you have. Because this is a retirement-focused book, we will focus on the Aged Widow benefit (as opposed to the Child in Care, Widow, or Disabled Widow Benefit) and the rules that surround it.

Prior to 2000, the retirement earnings test applied to people who worked any time between the ages of 62 and 70. People who worked past full retirement age often did not or were not able to claim benefits until they actually retired. As a result, approximately 15% of widows currently on Social Security's benefit rolls have Delayed Retirement Credits included in their widow's benefit. [6]

With the advent of the Senior Citizens Freedom to Work Act in 2000, the earnings test now no longer applies once you reach full retirement age. As a result, 16.7% of men who retired prior to the act received at least one Delayed Retirement Credit, but that percentage falls to only 2.8% of men born between 1935 and 1936, which is the first group to retire under the new rules about being able to work and collect benefits once you reach full retirement age. [7]

Who Dies First?

If you are married, at the death of the first spouse, the survivor receives the higher of his or her own benefit, or the *benefit of the deceased*, which may have been reduced if the deceased claimed early or increased by Delayed Retirement Credits if the deceased claimed late.

This is an incredibly important concept when making your initial election decisions because, in effect, claiming early reduces not only your own benefit but also the benefit paid to your survivor! The widow's benefit is, therefore, especially important to women because currently, 98% of the aged widows on Social Security's benefit rolls are women whose husbands died before they did. [5]

If a husband who is the higher wage earner decides to take benefits early, his decision will have a negative impact on the survivor benefit that will be paid to his wife if he dies before she does. Since women tend to live longer than men, it is critical that couples consider the impact of the survivor's benefit in the election decision.

You can begin receiving Aged Widow benefits as early as age 60. However, those benefits will be reduced due to claiming early. For example, let's assume that George had a PIA of $2,000. His spouse,

Jennifer, is 60 when George dies. The Aged Widow's benefit Jennifer could receive is based both on when George *claimed* and when Jennifer *decides to claim* that benefit. So here are her options:

- If George died at his full retirement age of 66 and never elected, Jennifer would be able to claim up to the full $2,000. If Jennifer was 60 when she claimed, she would receive 71.5% of the benefit, or $1,430 per month. If she waited until her full retirement age of 66 to claim, she would receive the full $2,000.

- If George claimed at 62 and was receiving $1,500 (75% of his PIA) per month until his death at age 66, after he dies Jennifer would only be entitled to up to $1,500 under the basic rule just outlined. However, in this case, there is another provision that would impact her benefit amount. It is known as the "Widow Limit," which caps a widow's benefits at the higher of the amount of the deceased spouse's benefit—or 82.5% of the deceased spouse's PIA. If Jennifer elected her widow's benefit at age 60, she would still receive the maximum reduction—down to $1,430 per month, but if she waited to 66, the most she could receive is $1,650, not the entire $2,000. In this case, Jennifer would not want to delay taking her widow's benefit past her age 62 and 4 months because it would not increase any further due to the Widow's Limit.

- If George began receiving Social Security at age 70, his benefit would have been $2,640. If he died one month later, Jennifer would receive up to $2,640 provided she claimed her Aged Widow's benefit at 66—or $1,887 per month if she claimed at age 60.

If you receive widow or widower's benefits, you may also switch to your own retirement benefits as early as age 62, assuming the amount will be more than you receive on your deceased spouse's earnings. In many cases, you can begin receiving one benefit at a reduced rate and then switch to the other benefit at the full rate when you reach full retirement age. And you can take a reduced benefit on one record, and later switch to a full benefit on the other record.

For example, a woman could take a reduced Aged Widow's benefit at 60 and then switch to her full (100%) retirement benefit when she reaches full retirement age. Or she could continue to get delayed credits on her own record past full retirement age and switch to her own benefit at age 70 (132%).

As noted earlier, many married couples that have lost a spouse or ex-spouse don't realize they are entitled to any part of the deceased's retirement benefits, let alone that they can create plans to maximize both their own retirement benefit and their widow or widower's benefits.

Here's an example: Bess is currently 65 years old; she'll turn 66 in nine months and her Social Security retirement benefit will be $1,800 per month. Her ex-husband Dan (they have been divorced for several years) just turned 66 last year and claimed his Social Security benefit of $1,800 per month.

If Dan dies suddenly, Bess has a couple of options. First, since they were married for more than ten years at the time of their divorce and she has not remarried, she is allowed to take as a widow's benefit *all* of what Dan was collecting under his retirement benefit, if she takes it at her full retirement age. Dan had remarried a year ago, so his current wife is also entitled to a widow's benefit! Realistically speaking, this means it would be possible for a 20-year-old person to remarry every ten years and a day leading up to full retirement age, die before actually getting there, and, if those four ex-spouses did not remarry, they could all be collecting widow's benefits! But we digress. Let's return to our actual example.

Bess reaches 66 and decides she's not ready to retire. If she doesn't claim her widow's benefit, she is simply leaving money on the table. The reason is this: She doesn't get any delayed credits for not taking her widow's benefit. If she waits, she is simply missing out on getting her monthly benefit checks. If her own benefit is higher, she can file for only the widow's benefit and let her retirement benefits earn delayed credits until she finally does decide to pack it in and retire at age 70. Then she would get a 32% increase on her own benefit, or up to $2,640 plus COLAs, while still being able to collect $1,800 per month in the meantime. And that would definitely affect other decisions she would make regarding her overall retirement financial plan.

Widow's Benefit Caution

If you were widowed before retirement and take your widow's benefit at age 60, watch out! When you file for Medicare, Social Security will check to see if your own benefit is higher than the widow benefit you are receiving. If it is, they will generally encourage you to switch to the higher retirement benefit. If your own benefit is higher at age 65, it rarely makes sense to make the switch then.

Generally, a much better strategy would be to continue to collect only your widow's benefit until age 70 and get a much larger raise in your own benefit due to Delayed Retirement Credits.

PROTECTION FROM INFLATION

We've already touched on the potential impact of inflation on an individual's retirement nest egg. But along with taxes (which we'll discuss later in this book), inflation plays a significant role in determining whether your money will last as long as you do. It should play a key part in your overall retirement planning. Ignore it at your peril.

Here's a look at what can happen: In a previous example, we introduced Jack who is an above-average wage earner and his wife, Jane, an average wage earner. They are both retiring at age 62. They will need

$65,000 a year in after-tax income adjusted annually for inflation to live on in their retirement. They have saved about $600,000 in IRAs but have no additional savings accounts or other assets besides their home.

If Jack takes his benefit at age 62, he will get $1,544 per month based on his lifetime earnings. If Jane takes her benefit at 62, she will get $1,163 per month based on her earnings record. Assuming their IRAs continue to grow at a rate of 6% per year and inflation grows above Social Security's 2.8% estimate at, say, 4%, assuming a 6% annual rate of return in their retirement accounts, Jack and Jane would fully exhaust their accounts by the time they reach age 80, leaving their Social Security providing them with only 50% of their needed income each month thereafter to live on. Not a pretty sight. They will be forced to curb their lifestyle and alter their financial plans dramatically.

Bringing the flexibility of the Social Security system to your strategizing is essential to building inflation protection into your overall plan. As it must be clear by now, such flexibility comes mostly after you have attained full retirement age. Only then are you able to file and suspend (file an application then immediately request a "voluntary suspension") to increase your benefits. Only then can you file a restricted application for a spousal benefit, delaying your own full retirement age benefit until later, as a way to both increase your income and enhance its purchasing power.

This is why full retirement age is such a critical marker; it's the point where you can put Social Security to greatest use in your planning to help you achieve your dreams of making your money last.

If both Jack and Jane were to delay filing for their own retirement benefit until age 70, with Jane electing only a spousal benefit at her full retirement age of 66, the couple would be able to spend down their IRA money early in retirement as a way to bridge the gap until their age-70 Social Security benefits kicked in.

Yes, they will have depleted their IRAs from $600,000 to about $170,000 by the time they turn 70. But they will also have "found" about $61,000 in the form of "added" spousal benefits that would otherwise have been lost had they both elected to start collecting their Social

Security at 62. As a result, that same IRA money will now last them until age 87. And even if they spent the entire balance in those IRAs, they would still have almost 88% (rather than 50%) of their required income coming in each month from Social Security.

Tap into Retirement Accounts (Scary but Smart)

If Jack and Jane were not comfortable spending so much of their retirement account balances early in retirement, they could do a split strategy in which Jane would claim her benefits early at 62, and Jack would claim a spousal benefit at 66 and then switch over to his own benefit at age 70.

If they followed this strategy, their IRAs would last them until they were 82, they will have accessed $45,000 of additional spousal benefits that would have been forfeited otherwise. Even if they drained their IRAs, they will still have about 71% of their annual income need covered by Social Security, and their total taxes paid would be about $108,000 (assuming the same tax brackets as the earlier example).

To clarify, total taxes paid over their lifetimes under the first scenario would be about $147,000 and total taxes paid under the second scenario about $80,000. This assumes the 2013 tax brackets married filing jointly, standard deductions, and personal exemptions also indexed at 4%,

If you were to have no assets other than Social Security, this would severely narrow your planning choices. But if you have other assets—such as a home, IRA, or other savings accounts—these strategies can greatly help you to reduce the tax liability on your Social Security, grow your lifetime income, and protect yourself against the whims of inflation.

SOCIAL SECURITY CONSIDERATIONS FOR GOVERNMENT EMPLOYEES

If you're a teacher, police officer, firefighter, government employee, or a spouse of those workers in a system that opted out of Social Security, you need to be aware of how the Government Pension Offset (GPO) and Windfall Elimination Provision (WEP) in Social Security will affect you.

While the GPO and WEP differ in who they affect and how they impact benefits, both are aimed at reducing Social Security benefits for people who receive a pension from work where they did not pay into the Social Security system.

Government Pension Offset (GPO) Provision Explained

The GPO provision reduces a government employees' Social Security spousal and survivor benefits by two-thirds of their government pension. Normally, the Social Security spousal benefit is equal to up to 50% of the retired or disabled worker's benefit and up to 100% of the deceased worker's benefit. GPO *reduces* the spousal and survivor benefit for spouses who also qualify for a government pension by two-thirds of the pension amount. If the pension from non-covered work is sufficiently large in comparison to the Social Security spousal benefit, GPO may eliminate the entire spousal or survivor benefit.

For example, Cindy worked in non-covered jobs her entire career and has a $3,000-a-month pension. Her husband, Bruce, worked sufficiently enough in Social Security–covered employment to be eligible for a $2,500 per month Social Security benefit if he elects at age 66. Cindy is, therefore, eligible for a spousal benefit of up to $1,250 under Bruce's work history.

However, under GPO, Cindy's spousal benefit is reduced to zero dollars because two-thirds of her pension ($2,000) is greater than her spousal benefit ($1,250). Upon Bruce's death, she would still get a survivor's benefit, but it would be only $500, rather than the $2,500 (at her full retirement age) she would otherwise get if the GPO did not apply.

Windfall Elimination Provision (WEP) Explained

The WEP reduces the Social Security benefits of people who qualify for both a Social Security benefit *and* a government pension based on their own earnings.

In order to understand how WEP affects benefits, you need to understand the basics of how Social Security benefits are calculated. As discussed, in general, a worker's monthly Social Security benefit is based on his or her thirty-five highest-paid years of Social Security–covered employment. The worker's earnings are indexed to wage growth to bring earlier years up to a current basis, then divided by thirty-five years, and divided again by twelve months per year to determine the Average Indexed Monthly Earnings (AIME).

Once a worker's AIME is established, the Social Security Benefit Formula is applied to arrive at the worker's PIA. That formula is a progressive one, which means workers with low average lifetime earnings will receive a larger proportion of their earnings as a Social Security benefit.

For an individual who worked in the private sector for, say, ten years then changed careers to become a public employee and paid no Social Security taxes, that person's AIME would be relatively low because his or her ten years of covered income would be averaged over thirty-five years. Therefore, the benefit formula would replace more of that individual's earnings at 90% than it would someone who spent his or her full thirty-five-year career in covered employment.

A worker's WEP reduction cannot exceed more than half of his or her pension. And workers who have thirty or more years of Social Security–covered employment are exempt from WEP. Nevertheless, more prospective retirees may be affected by GPO and WEP than even the government realizes.

If you're a teacher, police officer, firefighter, government employee, or the spouse of one, you should make sure your advisor is aware of how these provisions work, who they affect, and who can analyze your situation to see if there is a way for you to get more benefits rather than fewer.

Retire a Winner Checklist

Have you addressed the following issues?

☐ I am satisfied that my financial advisor understands all the uncommon strategies available to help me maximize my Social Security benefits.

☐ My advisor has explained to me in detail how and when I should claim my Social Security benefits.

☐ I have fully considered and compared all my sources of fixed income in retirement to determine whether to take Social Security first, or spend from other assets in order to delay Social Security. I understand how spousal benefits are coordinated with benefits on my own earnings record.

☐ I understand how survivor benefits work and have identified ways to make sure the survivor benefit is sufficient.

☐ I have considered my spouse and his or her life expectancy prior to choosing how to claim my Social Security benefits.

☐ I have calculated all the different claiming strategies for my spouse to determine the best strategy for electing when and how to claim Social Security benefits.

☐ I have considered the effects on the long-term income and legacy goals for retirement in maximizing Social Security benefits should I die before my spouse or vice versa.

☐ I have considered voluntary suspension as a viable option so that my spouse can begin to take his or her Social Security benefits while I continue to earn delayed credits.

☐ I have considered a "restricted application" to access spousal benefits while building Delayed Retirement Credits on my own record. I have also considered this option for my spouse.

MAKING INCOME LAST IN RETIREMENT (OR HOW TO SPEND ALL YOUR KIDS' INHERITANCE)

"It's not going to be your parents' retirement—rewarded at 65 with a gold watch, a guaranteed pension, and health insurance for life. For many Americans, retiring in this century is a mystery. Earlier generations of workers could rely on employer-provided pensions, but now many workers will need to rely on their own work-related and personal savings plus Social Security benefits. These savings have to last longer because Americans are living longer, often into their eighties and nineties."

—U.S. Department of Labor

ANALYZE THIS

Most Americans are by and large under-prepared for retirement. A 2009 survey by the Employee Benefit Research Institute (EBRI) suggested that only 44% of Americans have tried to calculate how much they need to save for retirement. The 2008 EBRI survey found that same percentage of people who tried to figure out their financial futures ended up changing their retirement savings plans and started socking away more moolah.

What is retirement planning about after all? If you follow the media or take advice from financial institutions and possibly even listen to your own (often misguided) financial advisors, you might think retirement planning is just about investing.

Although investing is part of it, retirement planning is really all about making sure you don't run out of money before you run out of life. It's all the other decisions, such as how long you work, how much you save, and how you use assets like Social Security, along with proper investment and protection strategies, that make the biggest impact on the success or failure of your plans.

A critical ingredient in creating any prudent retirement planning strategy is first of all to calculate the cost of your retirement. Of course, you can run a basic calculation yourself using one of the many online resources available on the Internet. But a basic calculation doesn't take into account the fact that it does not necessarily cost less to live in retirement as we have often been told.

Health care costs, entertainment, and travel are examples of some living expenses that can usually be expected to go up, not down, during our retirement years. And when you stop working, things like hyperinflation, new tax hikes, and bear markets can severely impact your buying power by eroding the value of your accumulated nest egg. That's why it is always important to look at retirement planning from a liability standpoint.

Types of liabilities should be considered as follows:

- *Necessary* living expenses. These would be housing, food, transportation, medical and other insurance, clothing, and the like.
- *Discretionary* expenses. Consider costs for entertainment, travel, and dining out.

Each type of expense will have unique cost of living increases that must be accounted for. This will require calculating the difference between the amount of income you can *expect* in retirement and the figure you may *need*. The deficit figure between the two is the gap you will have to fill in order to produce sufficient income to live on for the rest of your life.

Use the My Living Expenses Worksheet included in the Resources at the back of this book for itemizing your living expenses so that your financial advisor will be able to help you determine the deficit you will have to make up.

During retirement, most of you will have guaranteed sources of income, such as Social Security and possibly variable income sources as withdrawals from your savings. In order to determine what your deficit may be, you must start your planning, not conclude it, with a Social Security analysis and see what that tells you.

This upfront analysis can spell the difference between the creation of a good retirement plan that will go the distance with you or a poor one that might fall irretrievably short. It requires that you run through all the different claiming strategies available in order to determine the one that's best for you. Only then will your financial advisor be able to integrate that strategy into an overall framework designed to meet your financial needs in retirement to last you as long as necessary.

Let's look at Sam and Samantha to see what a Social Security Timing analysis suggests their optimum claiming strategy will be.

Sam was born in 1958; Samantha in 1957, so they were ages 55 and 56 in 2013, respectively. Their goal is to be able to stop working when Sam turns 60 and Samantha turns 61. As of 2012 they had accumulated $800,000 in total savings toward their retirement, much of it in tax-deferred investments such as their 401(k)s at work. They've estimated they'll need to bring in a net after-tax amount of $72,000 a year to live on comfortably in their retirement years.

A major expense for this couple will be the income tax owed on all withdrawals from their retirement accounts. Let's see what that $72,000 in living expenses will look like in retirement.

Both Sam and Samantha were born with good genes, each coming from a family with a history of longevity. Samantha's mother and grandmother are both still alive and well, so we'll project Samantha's life expectancy to be around 100. Statistics show that women live longer than men. We'll say that Sam's life expectancy is slightly less.

They are still a few years away from their desired retirement age, but that doesn't mean they should put off running some numbers. Will their estimated figure of $72,000 annually actually sustain them in their retirement, or will they run out of money before they run out of life?

What many Americans do at this stage is to contact Social Security and see how soon after they hang up their work shoes they can start claiming benefits and to hold off dipping into their pension money and other assets as long as possible. In other words, they begin by asking, "If I start claiming at 62, the amount of money I'll receive until I turn 66 is going to be X amount of dollars, but if I want to get $1,000 more a month by waiting until I'm 66, how long do I have to get that extra money before I will have gotten as much out of the system as I possibly could?"

As we've noted in a previous chapter, this is called a break-even analysis and may be insufficient in determining an optimal Social Security claiming strategy. Yes, single people can use a simple break-even calculator to determine how long they would have to live to make waiting worthwhile. But for married couples, the decision is much more complex.

Enterprise level tools (professional calculators and metrics) used by some financial advisors have the ability to handle most of those nuances. Once you reach full retirement age, you have the option to restrict your application to exclude certain benefits. If a benefit is excluded, it will continue to build Delayed Retirement Credits.

But Sam and Samantha have a financial advisor who is helping to steer them in the right direction. To make a proper determination about how long their money will last them with any degree of confidence that this scenario will actually play out, they must consider the impact on their retirement income of *all* their assets working together. This involves conducting several analyses, but it begins with a look at what maximizing Social Security benefits versus grabbing benefits as soon as they are available can do to enhance a financial plan's long-range probability of success.

The Risk Is Living Too Long (Not Dying Too Soon)

If your only goal is to get as much money out of the system as you possibly can as fast as you can, you can do that, but if your goal is to make sure *all* the financial resources you have last as long as you do, Social Security shouldn't be looked at in "break-even" terms.

You should take into account how best it can be utilized in conjunction with every other asset you have in affecting the probability of success that you will have the income you will need for the rest of your life.

It's not about how quickly you can get the money out and collecting as much as possible before you die because, as we've written, the risk is not dying too soon in retirement; the risk is living too long in retirement and not having enough money to last you because you were shortsighted and took your benefits early.

By analyzing their election options and combination of options as a married couple, Sam and Samantha are able to see what their optimal claiming strategy should be. Then they can base their decision when to start claiming benefits on hard numbers not on some ephemeral "break-even" point or hope-for-the-best guesswork.

For their analysis, Sam and Samantha want to be conservative in their estimate of future COLAs, so they use an expected Cost of Living Adjustment of 1.5%. After performing the analysis, Sam concludes that his best option is to begin benefits at his full retirement age of 66 years and 8 months. But rather than elect to receive his full retirement age benefit at that time, he will file a restricted application for his lesser-per-month spousal benefit instead.

This strategy will deliver him $1,453 a month (his spousal benefit), and all the while he's collecting that, his delayed full retirement age benefit will continue to grow at a guaranteed 8% a year. At age 70, he will then switch to his full retirement age benefit, which by then will have grown to $4,417, considerably more than if he'd elected early and sought to "break even."

Meanwhile, the same analysis of their Social Security claiming options has revealed that Samantha's optimum strategy is to take her retirement benefit at age 67 years and three months, then to immediately suspend that benefit, which will allow her to get Delayed Retirement Credits of 8% per year. When she turns 70, she will then request her retirement benefit to start, at which time this benefit will have grown as well—in her case to $4,066 a month.

What their respective strategies for optimizing Social Security will achieve for Sam and Samantha is this: Their total combined benefits are going to be almost $8,500 a month. If Sam lives to 95, he will have collected almost $1,681,000 in benefits. If Samantha lives to age 100, she will have collected $1,816,000 in benefits.

If you were to think about those benefit amounts in terms of how much they would need to have today to provide the same amount of income, you would be looking at a figure of about $2,225,000. This figure contrasts with the approximately $1,608,000 they would receive over time if they each claimed benefits at early as age 62—or more than a half-million-dollar difference over a long life.

Still, the question of whether their goal of $72,000 a year is now more likely, just as likely, or, perhaps, less likely to sustain them given their projected life expectancies has not been completely answered. A review of their investment portfolio is next. Together with their advisor, they will want to see how their other assets are currently allocated in order to determine what, if any, adjustments need to be made in that allocation given their Social Security strategy.

Although no single investment strategy guarantees profits or safeguards against loss, the idea is to determine what their required rate of return is to achieve their goals. Each family will have its own unique required rate of return, an absolute rate of return, not a relative benchmark, such as the Standard & Poor's 500 Index.

Many retirees may not need to take the investment risk of a portfolio comprised solely of stocks. Once the required rate of return is figured, the proper asset allocation can be determined.

The idea here is to get a fix on what Sam and Samantha's holdings should be, such as large and small companies, domestic and international stocks, bonds, real estate, cash, and other instruments and how those holdings should be apportioned. In other words, to find out how much *risk* their portfolio needs to take versus how much *reward* it can produce.

Let's say a review reveals their portfolio's risk/reward ratio is currently skewed in the direction of just slightly more risk than necessary. To make their asset allocation strategy more balanced and efficient, they now have the option to keep their potential return higher than their required rate of return or reduce their risk by altering their allocation. Or they can decide that the current imbalance is so slight that they choose to do nothing.

What's their best option? Having maximized Social Security first, they now have a critical piece of information they didn't have before to help them in making the best decision.

For simplicity's sake, the slight imbalance in the risk/reward ratio of their portfolio indicates they have a fairly high probability of success that their money will last as long as they do even if they make no changes at all to their current investment allocation and planning strategy. Perhaps with some minor adjustments in the allocation of their portfolio investments to bring their risk/reward ratio more comfortably into balance, they could push their probability of success even higher—for an even *bigger* win.

Without considering the optimal Social Security piece of their asset puzzle, Sam and Samantha would have had less input on how much risk their advisor would have to place on some of their investments to make up for any potential shortfall. By analyzing their Social Security options, they now have a better idea of how much risk they could comfortably afford to back away from and still make up for that shortfall.

Strike the Right Balance

Social Security is a form of "social insurance"—a fixed stream of income guaranteed for life. Some may ask, "Why bother with Social Security planning at all and not just allocate my portfolio with lots of annuities for retirement?"

An annuity may not provide the degree of protection that in most cases you will need to withstand the winds of inflationary change (more on that, later). It's true that annuities have evolved considerably over the years to address this problem. Today, a retiree can elect to have his or her monthly payments increase at rates ranging up to 6% per year. Alternatively, inflation-linked life annuities can be purchased.

Both kinds of inflation protection entail receiving lower initial payments, but they grow over time. However, you can erode your probability of success if your portfolio allocation is weighted too heavily toward any asset without proper regard to making sure that income stream will last. In other words, you can be too over-invested in one area and too under-invested in another.

It's critical to consider all sides of the equation in order to come up with the proper prescription, which is one that achieves the right balance not just between risk and reward but also between income and inflation protection.

The integration of Social Security into portfolio planning will help you and your financial advisor achieve a more balanced portfolio in all these vital areas, thereby helping increase your plan's long-term probability of success.

The integration of the proper Social Security claiming strategy with the proper asset allocation formula can make a major difference. In order to be able to integrate the proper Social Security claiming strategy into your overall financial planning strategy, the Social Security piece must be plugged in *first*. Before claiming, you and your advisor need to consider the allocation or re-allocation of the other assets in your investment portfolio. By chasing after income that you may not need to sustain your post-retirement lifestyle, you could actually be putting your assets at unnecessary risk and wind up reducing your plan's probability of success.

If you know through proper Social Security planning that you'll be able to increase your amount of fixed income in retirement to the tune of $131,000, as Sam and Samantha discovered in our example, this will allow you to take the pressure off the underlying investments in your portfolio and what those investments have to achieve in order to make your money last as long as you do.

Will Your Assets Cover Your Liabilities?

Proper asset allocation for retirement demands an approach similar to that of "liability-driven investing," a term large pension fund managers and large pension endowment firms use to determine the chances of whether the money they're thinking of investing to fund a liability will actually be there at some point in the future.

You must ask the same questions they do: What are my liabilities—what do I need to pay for year in and year out? Which of those liabilities will inflate? Which will not inflate (such as my mortgage)? Will some inflate at a faster rate than others?

Each asset must be singled out and assessed separately from a "liability-driven planning" perspective so that you can reasonably assume that the money you need will be there for you at some point in the future—and will last as long as you do.

There's a real tipping point between taking on too much risk or too little that could change your probability of success. Not until you know how to maximize Social Security will you be able to judge that tipping point with a higher degree of confidence and know how to re-position your portfolio to best meet your long-term income needs.

STRESS TESTING FOR INFLATION AND OTHER BUGABOOS

Let's consider the planning of another couple and subject it to a series of "stress tests" to get a more detailed view of their plan's probability of success as it strives to cope with different variables. Like Sam and Samantha in the previous example, Andre and Jasmine also want to have a net after-tax monthly income of $72,000 a year in their retirement.

Andre and Jasmine are now 64 years old and plan to retire next year when they turn 65. The Single Life Expectancy tables in the Resources section at the back of this book show that people their age today can expect to live an average of about 20 years in retirement—or until they're 82, maybe even 83. Keeping in mind that this couple is in good health and has a history of family longevity, we have agreed to plan for a twenty-five-year retirement time horizon, or to age 90. What level of living expenses might they expect in retirement?

Using some basic assumptions such as a 3.5% growth in the inflation rate over the twenty-five-year period of their retirement, we'll say that Andre and Jasmine would need to have about $3,078,653 in order to pay their living expenses and to not run out of money before they run out of life.

They have already done their Social Security planning and decided upon a claiming strategy that will contribute $22,000 annually to their retirement at full retirement age. To this they will be able to add another $40,000 a year from the employer-sponsored 401(k) pension plans they have at work. For this example, we'll index their combined income from these two sources in retirement at 3% and put the couple in a 25% tax bracket.

Based on these assumptions, Social Security and their pensions will account for $1,846,494—or 60%—of the projected $3,078,653 they will need to pay their living expenses in retirement and to not run out of money. This leaves a 40% deficit they will need from other capital assets they have to make up the difference.

Can You Pass This Stress Test?

It's important to keep in mind that, for some of you, it may be true that you will need less money in retirement, but this is not always the case. You'll need help taking your basic calculation a step further and applying it to a series of stress tests as well. Stress tests are simulations of economic and market conditions that can affect investments.

Additionally, Andre and Jasmine have Individual Retirement Accounts (IRAs). We'll say they have accumulated, as of this year, a combined total of $902,923 in their IRAs. This amount will likely keep growing after they retire—let's say at a rate of 5%—into a projected nest egg of $948,069 in 2013.

With a total retirement cost of $3,078,653, net retirement income sources of $1,846,494 and a projected nest egg of $948,069, allowing for total capital withdrawals (distributions) from the latter two sources of $1,575,522 after taxes, their income and assets will likely cover 111% of their total retirement costs! In other words, they will have successfully funded their entire retirement and still have some assets remaining to pass on to their heirs. Their future looks bright indeed. But …

In this instance, the "but …" is that they and their advisor are relying on linear rates of return each and every year, which may not happen. They have not yet considered the impact some of those familiar bugaboos such as inflation, potential market downturns, or health care events can have on the cost of their retirement and the purchasing power of their income.

For an idea of what the impact might be, their financial advisor will want to run a series of different simulations—called stress tests—reflecting different economic and market conditions on their savings over time. From the results, Andre and Jasmine will be able to more accurately measure their degree of confidence that their retirement plan can succeed under a wide variety of conditions.

Here are some scenarios:

- **Inflation:** What if inflation were to rise above our original assumption of 3.5% to 5% during their retirement? Stress testing the impact of that 1.5% jump in the rate of inflation on their portfolio under many possible futures reveals a percentage probability of success for their portfolio. At a 5% inflation rate, the trial runs indicate a probability of success of 99% that they will successfully be able to weather the impact of a spike in inflation to 5% on their portfolio assets during their retirement years. You can't beat those odds.

- **Market Downturn:** Introducing random market volatility into the equation helps illustrate that investment markets can have a distinct impact on their future plans as well. What if Andre and Jasmine were to lose, say, 20% of their savings in two consecutive years as the result of a plunge in the market similar to what many retirees experienced following the "Crash of 2008," and then the market doesn't immediately recover? A run-through of 500 trials in this instance would point to an overall probability of success of 24% that their portfolio will successfully be able to weather such a loss. All in all, those are pretty good odds too. Andre and Jasmine should have big smiles on their faces. But …

- **Health Care:** They should keep in mind that there is another *huge* bugaboo lurking out there ready to play havoc with the survival of their income. If fact, it's likely to be the most potentially damaging of all—that elephant in the room that most people are uncomfortable thinking about, let alone talking about and planning for. Yet its potentially negative impact on the sustainability of a couple's assets can be greater than inflation and market volatility (and taxes, which we'll cover in the next chapter) *combined!* We're speaking, of course, about *health care costs.* These *must* be planned for as well.

Biggest Risk: Long-Term Care

The National Academy of Elder Law Attorneys has compared the risk of financial devastation brought on by the need for extended care in a hospital or nursing home with the risk of financial devastation brought on by a major automobile accident or a house fire.

According to that study, the rates of risk were these: automobile accident: 1 out of 240 [0.4%]; house fire: 1 out of 1,200 [0.08%]; long-term care: 1 out of 2 [50%]. Further research has found that the worst-case scenario in terms of financial burden involves entering a nursing home and that the odds of a person needing extended care in a nursing home at age 65 or older are 49%, and grow to 56% for those 85 or older.

These statistics can be disconcerting, especially for those who have not planned what they will do in the event they or their spouse needs this type of care.

Advances in medical care have increased today's life expectancies substantially. With those advances, the chances have also increased the possibility that, as they grow older, Andre or Jasmine may become frail and need some form of extended at-home or nursing home care. Would their portfolio be able to sustain an extra monthly bill for such care if the need arises? Many families exhaust their funds after just a few short months in a nursing home.

Caregiving Is a Family Affair

Extended care is not a "you" problem, it is a "them" problem, meaning it is your family that will provide this care. And if you don't allocate some money in your retirement portfolio to pay for it, you and your family may wind up allocating everything.

This is not a risk proposition. It's a consequence proposition. Extended care is all about consequences—and how severe those consequences may be emotionally, physically, and financially to the well-being of family members providing the care.

Projecting ahead a decade or so, let's assume that Andre is now 75 years old and needs extended care for a period of four years. We'll assume also that the cost of his care in today's dollars will be about $180 daily, or about $65,700 a year—a figure that is likely to grow at a rate of 5% each year to $123,887 in the last year of his extended care need.

His and Jasmine's savings and assets, which they had expected to live on in retirement, may be used up much sooner than otherwise anticipated under these circumstances. Just how quickly might their resources vanish? Let's assume they have $500,000 of assets left in their portfolio when they are 75. Then the need for extended care arises. Assuming their assets will continue to grow at 5% annually and that withdrawals from those assets will face no tax whatsoever due to medical expense tax deductions, Jasmine would expect to have only about $87,000 remaining, and considerable remaining life expectancy to boot.

In addition to the possibility of extended care, calculating the cost of their retirement needs also must take into account the unpleasant topic of what would happen to Jasmine if Andre (who is the primary "bread winner" in this scenario) were to die prematurely.

The passing of one spouse does not necessarily mean the living expenses of the surviving spouse will automatically drop by 50%. They may remain the same, in which case Jasmine's income may not be sufficient to last her for the duration of her retirement.

How much of her future income could be lost if Andre dies suddenly this year? Let's say he was earning $125,000 per year. This lost income would cause her to have to spend other resources for living expenses in the final year of work possibly causing a shortfall for her own retirement. In addition she will receive less in Social Security since the smaller of their Social Security amounts will go away.

There may also be life-only pensions or annuities that could stop, all making it difficult for Jasmine to have the retirement she and Andre had planned for. The point is the need to plan for a premature death carries well beyond the working years, and unless it is properly factored into your retirement plan, retirement goals and dreams could be destroyed.

As you can see from all these possible scenarios, calculating the cost of retirement is not just a matter of running one set of numbers. A variety of numbers and considerations need to be taken into account and then integrated into your calculation—as well as into your overall plan. If you don't, the all-too-common result may be that you'll end up missing out on the "golden" part of your golden years.

Retire a Winner Checklist

Have you addressed the following issues?

☐ I have itemized all my necessary and discretionary living expenses so that my financial advisor will be able to help me determine the deficit I need to make up to meet my retirement income goal.

☐ I have planned accordingly to be able to take my Social Security benefits and still have "spendable" income that is in line with my personal needs without incurring unnecessary or excessive taxes on my Social Security or other income.

☐ I have integrated my best Social Security claiming strategy into my overall retirement income plan to determine if that strategy is an appropriate fit with my overall goals.

☐ I have made a determination of how delaying or filing for Social Security benefits early will affect both my current and future net "spendable" income needs in retirement.

KEEPING A SHARP EYE ON TAXES (DO YOU REALLY WANT TO PAY MORE THAN YOU NEED TO?)

BEWARE THE "STEALTH TAX"

As financial advisors, we are often surprised by the number of prospective retirees who come to us for planning and are shocked when we tell them that Social Security benefits are *taxable*. In fact, we once had a client who naïvely believed that once people retired, they were exempt from paying any taxes at all anymore. Not so. The only escape from taxes is death. And sometimes even that doesn't work.

About one-third of people who get Social Security will have to pay income taxes on their benefits. We call this the "stealth tax" because it comes in under the radar, and therefore a lot of people don't even see it coming until it's too late to do anything about it. It's almost like a double tax triggered in a very narrow window. You have to plan ahead for it—and that means understanding how taxes work in retirement.

Money can be taken away more easily than any other asset. Physical assets such as a painting, antique car, jewelry, collectibles, artifacts, land, or a home must be stolen or sold for you to lose them. But this is not true of money. You can lose money legally, and you can lose a lot of it without even knowing.

Taxes are one of the most serious wealth-eroding forces you face. The government uses tax revenue to operate, but the government is constantly changing. Tax laws are constantly changing as well. This means that no one really knows what the future tax laws will be. Since tax laws in the future are uncertain, any financial plan using today's tax laws to try to predict future outcomes may ultimately prove invalid and unreliable.

Nevertheless, a fundamental part of any financial plan is the need for a strategy to help prevent or minimize the effect of income taxes on your wealth. If you do not have such a plan, you can lose significant amounts of money that you may never be able to recapture. There are many income-tax-saving concepts you can use. Unfortunately, most people do not use any, and many use the wrong ones.

Tax-deferral is not a powerful weapon against income taxes; it only delays them. Many retirement savings plans today such as the 401(k) or IRA use this tax-deferred approach, and many people will be disappointed by it when they retire. Many people simply ignore the steps they can take to help save on taxes. If you spend more time trying to hold on to your money instead of spending time trying to find an investment to make money, you will be much better off.

Tax Allocation versus Asset Allocation

Different account types are taxed differently. A qualified Roth IRA distribution is tax free; most IRA or 401(k) distributions are taxable as ordinary income. Life insurance cash value withdrawals come out first in–first out; deferred annuity withdrawals generally come out last in–first out; and immediate annuities offer an exclusion ratio. Taxable accounts are taxed as earnings and are realized either as dividends, capital gains, or interest.

The idea of tax allocation is to use the differing tax properties of the different types of accounts to your advantage. If that's Greek to you, you're not alone. Well-educated financial advisors pay special attention to tax treatment of accounts because it is an important value-add for their clients.

By properly structuring your tax allocation strategy in retirement, you may improve your probability of success in achieving all the income that you need to keep up with potentially higher taxes and inflation throughout your retirement years and to not run out of money than with just asset allocation alone. Remember: you don't wear a seatbelt in your car every day because you think you're going to get into a crash. You wear it in case you do.

The same philosophy must be incorporated into all your money decisions: You hope nothing ever happens, but if it does, you need a plan that is designed to work under that scenario. If sound financial planning were merely a matter of discipline to save and invest money over the long run, everyone's financial plan would work successfully. Unfortunately, it is simply not that easy: many financial plans do not contain all the components that will help determine whether you are successful.

Social Security has unique issues when it comes to taxes. To determine the taxability of your Social Security, you must take into consideration your provisional (also known as your combined) income, which is arrived at by taking 50% of your Social Security benefits and adding that figure to all the other taxable and tax-free interest income you receive in retirement.

If you're a married couple filing jointly, fifty cents of every dollar of provisional income above the first threshold of $32,000 per year is taxable as ordinary income. For each dollar of provisional income above the second threshold of $44,000, an additional thirty-five cents of every dollar is taxable as ordinary income, up to the maximum of 85% of your Social Security benefits taxable as ordinary income. For singles, the respective thresholds are $25,000 and $34,000.

There are some so-called experts who believe that since 85% of all Social Security will be taxed as ordinary income once singles and couples hit these retirement income thresholds, tax on Social Security cannot be avoided. This is not true. By thinking strategically about how best to allocate and spend your assets, it's possible to have much more "spendable" income than provisional income during retirement—thereby keeping your Social Security assets untaxed or taxed at a lower rate.

Social Security income is not taxed the same as IRA income. This means you may be able to reduce your taxes by choosing higher Social Security income and lower IRA income when you develop your strategy for taking retirement income.

Here's how that works: Suppose you have two separate accounts: an IRA worth $500,000 and a non-qualified joint account worth $500,000 with no capital gains exposure. [Non-qualified means the funds are not in any IRA or other "tax-qualified" plan. And just to clarify, you pay capital gains tax on appreciated assets only when you sell them.]

Traditional retirement planning teaches us that we should spend our interest first and preserve our principal. That thinking, however, means that if you were to draw 5% from each account each year, the entire 5% (assuming 5% interest is annually earned on the account) would be included not only in your provisional income but also in your Adjusted Gross Income (AGI). [Your Adjusted Gross Income includes all income paid to you in a given year adjusted downward by specific deductions such as retirement account contributions and reported on your annual 1040 income tax return.] Likewise, the 5% withdrawal from your IRA would also be included in your provisional income as well as in your taxable income (5% of $1 million [$500,000 + $500,000] is $50,000 per year).

If you are married, and you add half of your Social Security benefits to that $50,000, it would put you well in excess of the $44,000 threshold for couples. Many advisors assume this would mean 85% of your Social Security is taxable. But that's not the case. In this example, assuming married-filing-jointly tax status, $28,100 (or 70% of your total benefit) would be taxable, according to IRS Publication 915. [8]

Properly allocating the spending of assets can avoid such high taxation and reduce the amount of withdrawal necessary to meet your living expenses. Taking the facts of this example, but now applying it to a single person, you may still have options to reduce taxes. In this example, if you were 62 years old, you could set aside $330,000 of the $500,000 in a taxable account and begin to spend that money, drawing principal and interest first.

Assuming a 5% rate of return, that $330,000 would be totally exhausted by age 70½ when required minimum distributions begin on your IRA. [Minimum distributions are the minimum amount you must take out of your Individual Retirement Account (IRA) starting at age 70½] Over that period of time you would have received the same $50,000 per year in "spendable" income. However, less than $10,000 of that would be included in your provisional income, thereby allowing you to stay below the $25,000 threshold for singles that causes your Social Security to become taxable.

A Point about Pensions

If you get a pension from work where you paid Social Security taxes, that pension will not affect your Social Security benefits. However, if you get a pension from work that was not covered by Social Security—for example, the Federal civil service, some state or local government employment, or work in a foreign country—your Social Security benefit may be reduced.

For the next five years, this structure would allow you to have $90,000 in tax-free "spendable" income. You would be building up a tax liability in your IRA, for example, which you will be forced to tap into at age 70½, but that may be an acceptable trade-off. The key to creating a sufficient income stream is determining which accounts should be tapped in order to minimize your *lifetime* tax burden, not your tax burden today.

This is a simplified example, but it allows you to see how through proper planning you may be able to reduce your tax bill during retirement, thus giving you either more money to spend or allowing you to withdraw a smaller amount and still have the same net "spendable" money as you would have had drawing interest from both taxable and IRA accounts.

Social Security is an integral part of your retirement plan and must be considered in context with all other assets you hold either in IRAs or in non-qualified accounts. If you take IRA income first while delaying the start of your Social Security benefits, you're choosing to take higher lifetime Social Security benefits and lower lifetime IRA income.

Once you reach age 70 and start taking a much higher Social Security amount, you are taking one additional dollar in the form of Social Security income as opposed to IRA income—and not paying tax on that Social Security dollar "out of the box" (which is not true of the IRA dollar). Instead it goes into your provisional income at a 50% rate. So the retiree with IRA income (and lower Social Security) may pay taxes while the retiree receiving that income in the form of Social Security may not.

Here's another example of a Social Security planning and tax allocation strategy. Arthur is a 62-year-old teacher who expects to live to age 100 because he has longevity on his side. He is eligible for maximum Social Security benefits but instead wants to take his Social Security benefits at age 62 at a reduced amount of $27,000 per year. He also holds $500,000 in a taxable savings account and another $500,000 in an IRA. He requires $65,000 per year net of taxes to have a comfortable retirement and would like to be able to keep up with an estimated 4% inflation rate to sustain that amount.

If Arthur were simply to rely on asset allocation alone, a "Monte Carlo stress test" indicates he will have to place most of his assets into equities to achieve an 81% probability of success that he will not outlive his money. While this percentage may be acceptable for some, allocating most of his portfolio in equities at retirement is too risky for Arthur. Indeed it's too risky for most people at retirement and more than they're willing to commit. [A Monte Carlo simulation stress test is a problem-solving technique used to approximate the probability of certain outcomes by running multiple trial runs, called simulations, using random variables.]

So Arthur sits down with his financial advisor and together they come up with an alternate strategy to improve Arthur's probability of success while possibly cutting down his risk. First, instead of taking his Social Security benefits early, he could consider delaying them until he is age 70. This will allow his Social Security benefits to continue to accumulate at 8% per year, bringing the total yearly benefit at age 70 to $47,520.

He could also convert part of his IRA to a Roth IRA, paying tax on the converted amount but none thereafter even on compounded accumulation, and defer taking any income from the Roth until he's 70. Therefore, all income will be driven from the balance of the taxable investment, and since he is spending principal, there will be no income taxes due after the year of the initial conversion to a Roth IRA.

After Arthur turns 70, the advisor could target the distributions from the remaining traditional IRA to keep them plus any taxable Social Security under the standard deduction plus personal exemptions of the couple, then supplement the Social Security benefit with Roth IRA withdrawals, maintaining a tax-free retirement income.

Most people won't take the time to sit down and try to grasp the wealth-eroding factors that face them from taxation. It's understandable: The calculations can be confusing and trying to figure them out can be intimidating—not to mention almost as boring as watching paint dry. That's why you need a competent financial advisor with the expertise to help you maximize the wealth you have created using all tools and techniques available and necessary to help provide you with the highest probability of success that your goals, as defined by *you*, can be achieved.

As we've shown, a powerful part of these tools and techniques is tax reduction strategies. To make sure you are giving yourself the greatest chance of meeting your retirement goals, look at your current plan and see if you have these tools and techniques in place. If you don't, make it a goal to find out how these strategies might fit into your plan. And don't wait until the last minute to begin strategizing, or assume you know all the answers, as Rick did in this next case study—or you may give the taxman an edge.

Now that we've discussed tax options and dangers in retirement, let's look at two case studies to illustrate the details.

Case Study 1: Rick and Ethel

Rick was a successful small business owner who had recently sold his business of many years. He had recently turned 62 and had decided not to claim his Social Security benefits right away, which amounted to $21,000 a year. The stock market plunge of 2008 had put quite a dent in his other holdings, reducing the value of his taxable assets from $3 million to $1 million. He also had a tax-deferred IRA worth $800,000.

His wife, Ethel, had been a homemaker for much of their married life. She had just turned 59. Rick's health wasn't in the best of shape, but Ethel's was excellent. She boasted that her mom was still going strong at age 86, so there was no reason to believe she would not be able to enjoy a long, long retirement even if something happened to Rick.

Their income goal was $110,000 a year, beginning this first year of Rick's retirement, so they went to a financial advisor who specialized in retirement planning to see what reassurances he could offer them.

"If you had come to me sooner, we would have had a few more planning options," he told them, "but let's give your situation a look and see where you stack up."

He carefully reviewed all their assets and liabilities, then, after a short time, looked across his desk at them and said, "Look, I'm not going to mince words. You may have difficulty meeting your income goal for anywhere near the length of time you need." He paused, then said: "No, I take that back; you *will* have a problem."

Color drained from their faces.

The advisor went on to point out that in order for them to net $110,000 a year, they would need to bring in about $150,000 a year to cover their annual tax burden of about $40,000 ($110,000 plus $40,000 = $150,000). Part of the reason their tax burden was so high, the advisor explained, was because they lived in New York, which charged a state income tax on top of Federal income tax. But the real crux of the problem was the shortfall they would have to make up just to get their initial target of $9,167 a month coming in.

"You've got Rick's $21,000 a year in Social Security coming in," the advisor explained. "Subtract that amount from $110,000 and you're faced with a $7,417 per month shortfall that you will only be able to get to by pulling income from the $1.8 million you have in other assets. To cover the taxes on the withdrawals, you'll need to make up the shortfall. You'll have to take those withdrawals at a rate of 7.1% a year. Unfortunately, at that rate of distribution every year, all your assets except Social Security will be very quickly wiped out."

More color drained from Rick and Ethel's faces as they sat there searching the advisor's expression for some ray of hope.

"Is there *nothing* we can do?" Ethel asked finally.

The advisor was silent for a moment. Then he said, "I think I do see one opportunity."

Rick's face brightened ever so slightly. "What's that?" he asked.

"We've got to get that distribution rate down on your other assets and see that you have to pay no taxes for the next eight years."

Rick looked as if the advisor had just suggested they locate a pot of gold at the end of a rainbow.

"That's the only way to get the numbers in line with your needs," the advisor concluded. "But I think we can manage it."

Rick folded his arms and looked at the advisor skeptically. "You do know I'm an MBA, don't you?" he said.

"Of course, I do," the advisor replied. "It's right here in your information. However, your academic training was focused on tax-efficient *accumulation* of assets. My training is finding the most tax-efficient method of *distributing* assets."

Rick leaned forward in the chair, and said, "OK, we're all ears. Tell us what the magic solution is."

The advisor went on. "The first thing we have to consider is how Social Security income is taxed," he said. He looked at Rick. "Are you familiar with the term *provisional income?*"

"No, never heard of it. What is provisional income? And why is it important?"

"Well, if you understand provisional income and what causes Social Security to be taxed, there's a good chance you can avoid paying taxes on Social Security and everything else," the advisor said.

Rick gave him a look that said, "Show me."

"Rick, Ethel, part of provisional income is half of your combined sources of *fixed* income, which in your case is just Social Security, and 50% of $21,000 is $10,500," the advisor continued. "The provisional income limit for an individual that causes Social Security to be taxed is $32,000. So that leaves you $21,500 more you can net before your Social Security is taxed [$32,000 minus $10,500 = $21,500]."

The advisor paused for a second and then asked, "Now, what is *not* included in your provisional income is the principal on your investment income. And it's been drummed into all of us practically from birth that in retirement you absolutely, positively *do not dip into your principal*. Always spend down interest first, right?"

Rick nodded. "Yep, that's what my dad always said, and it seemed like good advice. Isn't it true?"

The advisor shook his head no. "The problem with such an approach is that interest is taxable," he explained. "But if you were to cut your $1 million of taxable money in half and move that $500,000 into that $800,000 bucket of tax-deferred money called your IRA, you will have more tax flexibility. You following?"

Rick and Ethel nodded quickly, intrigued at the direction in which the advisor was heading with his calculations.

"Now, if you were to spend down that $500,000 in taxable money between now and when you turn age 70½," the advisor continued, "and were to amortize at a 4% rate, it would all be used up in about eight years, but you will have been able to make up your $89,000 per year shortfall in the process (that's the $110,000 total income minus the $21,000 from Social Security). Add to it the $21,000 you have coming in from Social Security, and you would be able to hit your $110,000 a year goal. And because most if not all of what you'll be spending down during those eight years will be principal, you'll be paying almost *zero* in taxes all that time!" [Money is coming from a savings account in this example.]

Rick and Ethel looked at each other in astonishment. "I'll be damned," Rick said. "It will actually work, won't it?"

"Yes," their advisor replied with deep satisfaction. "I believe it will."

Even though their opportunity for creating a good retirement planning strategy had almost passed its "sell-by" date, Rick and Ethel—with some artful help from their advisor—managed to pull their plan from the fire and improve their long-term situation.

But had they not waited until the last minute to meet with that advisor, one who specialized in Social Security maximization techniques and retirement planning, they would have had much greater flexibility, more financial choices, increased leverage, and been able to put themselves on even firmer ground long term.

The lesson of their story is don't wait or you could wind up being too late—and seek the help of a professional if you need it.

"The Social Security program is a pact between workers and their employers that they will contribute to a common fund to ensure that those who are no longer part of the work force will have a basic income on which to live. It represents our commitment as a society to the belief that workers should not live in dread that a disability, death, or old age could leave them or their families destitute."

—President Jimmy Carter,
December 20, 1977

Case Study 2: Gene and Sally

Now here's the story of a very different couple. Gene and Sally planned ahead, and as a result the path they and the advisor were able to chart with a little tweaking here and there increased their plan's probability of success significantly.

Gene was 65 years old and his wife, Sally, was 61 when they went to see their advisor about their retirement plan. At the time, Gene was still working as a senior engineer, pulling in $100,000 a year. For much of their married life, Sally had been a stay-at-home mom, taking care of their children. But their children were now grown, and she works outside the home as an office assistant, making $30,000 a year.

This couple was extremely well prepared when they arrived at their advisor's office, having brought with them all pertinent documents, including a list of their various retirement account assets, which looked like this:

Gene's Accounts

401(k) (former employer) = $265,000
IRA #1 = $110,000
IRA #2 = $75,000
401(k) (current employer) = $125,000
IRA #3 = $65,000

Sally's Accounts

SIMPLE IRA = $50,000 [SIMPLE stands for Saving Incentive Match Plan for Employees—a type of tax-deferred, employer-provided retirement plan.]
IRA = $40,000

They have taken some very positive steps toward retirement, from contributing heavily to their tax-deferred 401(k)s to allocating their other assets in a way that was a very good fit with their age and circumstances. Gene was getting ready to retire and wanted advice on which accounts he should draw from at which points in order to make their money last. As Sally was on the cusp of retirement age, she wanted to know what strategy she should pursue as well.

Gene had been near the earnings cap for Social Security credits most of his working life, so his estimated benefit if he waited until his full retirement age of 66 to start claiming would be about $2,500 per month. As noted previously, Sally had stayed at home with their children for much of her adult life and had begun working outside the home much later, so her estimated Social Security benefit if she too continued to work to age 66 would be less—approximately $1,200 per month.

The couple knew they still had a few big expenses to deal with and wanted to establish how best to pay them off before retiring. For example, they had ten years and a balance of $105,000 left on their mortgage, while their house was valued at $220,000.

Also, once Gene retired and no longer needed private health insurance, health care coverage for Sally would continue to cost around $500 a month until she turned 65 and became eligible for Medicare like he was. They also knew that after that they could expect their total annual health insurance expense would be approximately $300 each per month, including parts A (no premium), B (about $100 a month), and D (about $30 a month) as well as a Medigap policy (roughly $120 a month), plus a cushion for out-of-pocket expenses.

They were likewise aware that health care costs have historically increased faster than general inflation, so they had planned for an estimated 5% increase in inflation on both his and her health insurance expenses, compared to 3% for normal living expenses. Further, they had bought long-term care insurance under their state's Partnership program to protect against a catastrophic expense in the form of extended care.

Gene and Sally's lifestyle would be considered moderate. They had become accustomed to living on about $65,000 a year after taxes and specific named expenses such as their mortgage. They wanted—and expected—to live a reasonably long and active but not extravagant lifestyle in retirement, including travel and new hobbies.

As already described, the cost of Gene's health care insurance would go down considerably when he went on Medicare, but Sally's out-of-pocket health care costs would continue to remain high for a number of years after Gene retired until she too reached 65 and was eligible for Medicare. So rather than a drop in their overall expenses, it looked as if their post-retirement expenses would be roughly the same as their pre-retirement expenses, at least for a period of time. This meant that basically what they used to spend on savings and taxes would, in retirement, be spent on lifestyle.

From a cash-flow perspective, this indicated that their total expenses would drop slightly in four years when Sally became eligible for Medicare and no longer needed private health insurance, then decrease even further in ten years when their mortgage was finally satisfied.

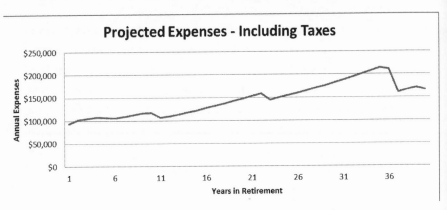

When they came to the advisor to actually finalize a plan, Gene and Sally had agreed after much discussion between them on the following course of action: Gene would retire at age 65 because he would then qualify for Medicare; at the same time he would start claiming his Social Security benefits. Sally would follow suit in four years when she turned 65.

However, upon closer examination of their respective assets and situation, the advisor suggested that while this strategy was indeed feasible, a few simple changes to it would greatly increase the working efficiency of their money over a longer period of time.

Here's how and why: If the couple were to claim their Social Security benefits at age 65 as planned, they would need to take the following withdrawals from their retirement accounts in order to maintain their $65,000-a-year lifestyle while covering all expenses and taxes.

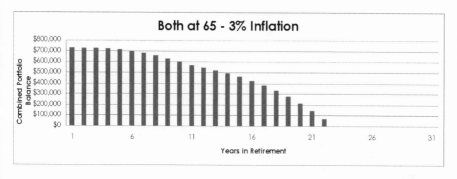

Assuming a 6% return on those assets, this pace of withdrawal would mean these accounts would be exhausted by the time Gene and Sally turned age 85 and 81, respectively. And once these sources of income were exhausted, the couple would then have only about 60% of their annual income requirement covered. So they began talking alternatives with their advisor, who recommended these simple changes the couple could make that could potentially both extend the life of their portfolio and protect them from outliving their savings:

- Gene would file for his Social Security benefits at age 70 (not 65). Delaying his benefits would allow him to get a 32% increase over his full retirement age benefit for a total benefit of $3,300, plus any cost of living increases.
- If Gene were to die before Sally, which is quite likely due to age and gender statistics, she would then be able to receive that same amount, again adjusted for cost of living, in survivor benefits.
- Sally should file for only her spousal benefit under Gene's earnings record when she reaches her full retirement age of 66. She will receive $1,250 per month plus any Cost of Living Adjustments.
- When Sally reaches age 70, she should file to receive her own Social Security benefit to replace the $1,250 spousal

benefit she had been taking. Her full retirement age benefit will have been increasing by 8% per year all this time, so instead of receiving what would otherwise have been her PIA of $1,200 a month, she will now receive about $1,584 a month, plus any COLAs.

Of course, with Gene retiring at age 65 but electing not to receive full benefits until age 70 and with Sally also retiring at age 65 but not taking any benefits until age 66, this strategy will, as a result of the postponement, create an income gap for the couple that will need to be filled.

In order to bridge that gap and be able to meet their after-tax spending need, Gene and Sally will have to take withdrawals from their IRA accounts, contrary to the standard financial services industry recommendation that such assets should never be tapped first. But now those accounts will be fully depleted by the time Gene is 92 and Sally 88. That's a big leap from being depleted at ages 85 and 81, respectively, if the couple had not altered their original plans.

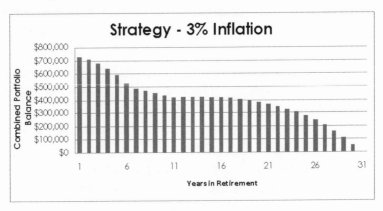

Furthermore, were either Gene or Sally to die early, the survivor would now receive $39,600 a year (plus COLAs) instead of only about $30,000 (plus COLAs), which would have been the case originally.

Additionally, as shown in the tax comparison, while the couple's taxes will be slightly higher in the first seven years of their retirement, those taxes will become drastically lower over time, in spite of the fact that Gene and Sally will have increased their monthly income from Sally's having claimed her spousal benefit (that would otherwise have gone unclaimed) while earning delayed credits on her own earnings record.

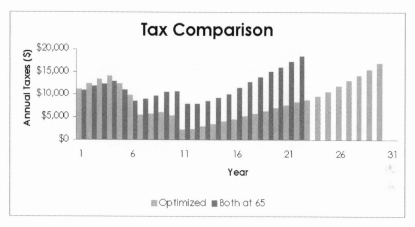

This tax comparison shows annual taxes paid, assuming brackets, personal exemptions, standard deductions inflating at 3%, rates staying the same within each bracket, and provisional income thresholds at current levels (not indexed).

Due to the small changes they've made at the suggestion of their advisor, even when Gene and Sally's IRA funds are fully exhausted, they will still have 90% (as opposed to 60%) of their necessary monthly income requirement covered, which is a substantial boost not just in the probability of success they will outlive their money, but also in their current and long-term abilities to plan for unforeseen expenses.

WHAT'S ACCEPTABLE TO YOU?

A key question that you should always ask alongside the traditional, "How long will my money last?" is this: "If it doesn't last (due to poor investment returns, health events, or other unforeseen circumstances), will I/we have enough inflation-adjusted income to live on?"

Prior to seeing their advisor, Gene and Sally would have had approximately 60% of their retirement income goals covered by their initial planning. After his slight changes to their plans, they can see that they will now have 90% of their lifetime income need covered. For Gene and Sally, 90% was an acceptable bottom line.

Your acceptable bottom line may vary. So when building your own retirement plan, you should always approach it from two angles: (1) What do you want your ideal retirement lifestyle to look like? and (2) What is the worst reduction in that ideal you are willing to tolerate? You should consider guarantees such as Social Security, annuities, or other inflation-protected lifetime income sources to help secure your acceptable bottom line.

Retire a Winner Checklist

Have you addressed the following issues?

☐ I have gone through all the calculations necessary to determine if delaying my Social Security benefits will allow me to convert to a Roth IRA and keep my tax bracket low.

☐ I understand the unique taxation provisions of Social Security benefits relative to my other assets and have identified any strategies associated with offsetting taxable income in retirement.

☐ I have met with my advisor and Certified Public Accountant to fully understand how much of my Social Security is going to be taxable and have included those calculations in my retiremen projections.

☐ I have calculated how much of my benefits will be taxable in determining when to take Social Security so I can maximize my "spendable" income.

6

GET IT RIGHT THE FIRST TIME

BEWARE: NO "DO-OVERS"

If you've read through the previous chapters thoroughly, it is evident by now that Social Security planning is very complex. It's a complicated business where one error can wind up losing you a serious amount of money.

Until December 2010, you had the ability to "fix a mistake" by filing a form 521 with the Social Security Administration and repaying past benefits. You could even take a tax credit or deduction for taxes you had paid on the benefits you had received. Now, however, you have only one year from your initial election to "withdraw" your application via a form 521.

As a result, making the right decision is now more important than ever. Unlike investing where a loss due to bad advice or an error in do-it-yourself judgment can be recovered from, given enough time, a mistake in claiming your Social Security benefits cannot be undone no matter how much time may pass.

That said, if you've read this far into this book and realize now that you wish you had gone a different route, you may still have options. Let's review them:

Option 1: Go Back to Work

If you are outside the twelve-month window and decide you want to go back to work between the ages of 62 and full retirement age (FRA), your benefits will be subject to the retirement earnings test. The 2013 earnings test exempt amount is $15,120 ($40,080 in the year you reach full retirement age). Social Security will withhold $1 in benefits for every $2 of earnings in excess of that amount ($1 for $3 in the year you reach full retirement age). *This is not a tax!*

Let's say you elected benefits at 62 and were receiving $1,800 as a monthly benefit (75% of $2,400) and now want to go back to work at 63 earning $90,000 per year ($90,000 - $15,120 = $74,880). Divide that by two and the earning penalty would be $37,440. Since that is greater than the total Social Security benefit of $21,600, you can request that your benefit be suspended during this period. Note: without the work income, Social Security rules preclude offices from voluntarily suspending benefits prior to full retirement age.

The reason we want to be very clear that the "earnings penalty" is not a tax is because Social Security would adjust the reduction on your benefits for each month in which you didn't receive a check due to the earnings test. If you actually received benefits for the twelve months you were 62, but then worked and did not receive any further benefits until age 66, Social Security would go back to your record and adjust your benefit upwards. They will treat it as if you had originally elected at 65 instead of 62, so you would then begin receiving a check for $2,240 plus any Cost of Living Adjustments that had accrued.

Option 2: Voluntarily Suspend

Here's another option for those who don't want to go back to work. Once you reach full retirement age, you can voluntarily suspend benefits. You simply need to call or visit a Social Security office and request a voluntary suspension. You can even call in advance of your full retirement age with instructions to suspend at FRA.

Here's where it gets interesting. See if you can follow the math here. By electing at age 62, you reduced your monthly benefit to 75% of what you would have received if you had elected at FRA. By suspending benefits at age 66, you will increase this monthly benefit by 8% per year until age 70, for a total of 32%. So if you increase 75% by 32% you get 99% (.75 x 1.32 = .99). In other words, you can take Social Security from 62 to 66, suspend from 66 to 70 and still get 99% of the benefit you would have gotten had you simply waited until full retirement age.

This should not be viewed as a claiming strategy, only as a means for minimizing the damage of a mistake. There are several reasons you wouldn't want to elect at 62 with the intent of suspending at FRA. First, if you die between 62 and FRA, your surviving spouse would be permanently stuck with a substantially reduced benefit. Second, you would forfeit any future option of claiming a restricted spousal benefit, because once you file for your own benefit, even if it is in suspension, your spousal benefit is reduced as if you were actually receiving your benefit. If your own suspended benefit is higher than your spousal benefit, you will not receive a spousal benefit.

Option 3: Maximize Benefits for a Spouse Who Has Not Yet Elected

If you have already elected benefits, but your spouse has not yet elected, you can identify the best of the remaining strategies for the spouse who has not yet elected. Often the election option that makes the most sense for the spouse in this context is not the one that would have made the most sense if considered in a vacuum.

Option 4: Buy Private Insurance

If you haven't noticed yet, much of this book is about risk management. Social Security planning for married couples generally involves using Social Security election strategies to minimize the inherent risks in retirement, such as outliving your money or the death of a spouse. Social Security is a unique tool for managing these risks.

That said, if it's too late to use Social Security as the tool to help you manage these risks, then consider insurance products designed to help manage the same risks.

These options may provide some relief from a poor decision, but, ideally, you would be better with planning before you make a mistake. This is a clear case where you may want to consider the help of an expert advisor who fully understands the different claiming strategies available to choose from and how to integrate the best strategy into your overall retirement plan to help your combined nest egg last as long as you do.

"America will always keep the promises made in troubled times a half century ago. [Social Security is] a monument to the spirit of compassion and commitment that unites us as a people."

—President Ronald W. Reagan,
April 20, 1983

NOTES

1. The Securities and Exchange Commission defines a "Ponzi" scheme as "an investment fraud that involves the payment of purported returns to existing investors from funds contributed by new investors." The scheme is named after Charles Ponzi who duped thousands of New England residents into investing in a postage stamp speculation scheme back in the 1920s by promising them a 50% return in just ninety days. This, of course, was impossible and led to his exposure for fraud.

2. SSA Publication No. 05-10029, Disability Planner: Social Security Protection If You Become Disabled, www.ssa.gov/dibplan/index.htm.

3. National Committee to Preserve Social Security & Medicare, www.ncpssm.org/ss_primer.

4. Munnell, Alicia H., Steven A. Sass, Alex Golub-Sass, and Nadia Karamcheva. "Unusual Social Security Claiming Strategies: Costs and Distributional Effects." Center for Retirement Research, Boston College, August 2009; http://crr.bc.edu/wp-content/uploads/2009/08/wp_2009-17-508.pdf.

5. www.ssa.gov/policy/docs/ssb/v70n3/v70n3p89.html
6. www.ssa.gov/policy/docs/ssb/v70n3/v70n3p89.html
7. www.ssa.gov/policy/docs/ssb/v70n3/v70n3p89.html
8. IRS Publication 915, Social Security and Equivalent Railroad Retirement Benefits, www.irs.gov/pub/irs-pdf/p915.pdf.

RESOURCES

SINGLE LIFE EXPECTANCY TABLES

The Social Security Administration has prepared the following "Period Life Table" for the population of people covered by Social Security. More highly educated and wealthier individuals tend to live longer on average.

The period life expectancy at a given age is the average remaining number of years expected prior to death for a person at that exact age, born on January 1, using the mortality rates for 2009 over the course of his or her remaining life.

You can get a basic estimate of your own life expectancy by finding your exact current age and adding the number in the appropriate column for male or female. Remember, this is a single life table. Couples may want to consider using a joint life calculator, such as the one available through the Society of Actuaries at www.soa.org/research/software-tools/research-simple-life-calculator.aspx. Other factors, of course, play into how long you will actually live.

SINGLE LIFE EXPECTANCY TABLES
PERIOD LIFE TABLE, 2007

Exact Age	Male Life Expectancy	Female Life Expectancy
0	75.38	80.43
1	74.94	79.92
2	73.98	78.95
3	73	77.97
4	72.02	76.99
5	71.03	76
6	70.04	75.01
7	69.05	74.02
8	68.06	73.03
9	67.07	72.04
10	66.08	71.04
11	65.09	70.05
12	64.09	69.06
13	63.1	68.07
14	62.12	67.08
15	61.14	66.09
16	60.18	65.11
17	59.22	64.13
18	58.27	63.15
19	57.33	62.18
20	56.4	61.2
21	55.47	60.23
22	54.54	59.26
23	53.63	58.29
24	52.71	57.32
25	51.78	56.35

Exact Age	Male Life Expectancy	Female Life Expectancy
26	50.86	55.38
27	49.93	54.4
28	49	53.44
29	48.07	52.47
30	47.13	51.5
31	46.2	50.53
32	45.27	49.56
33	44.33	48.6
34	43.4	47.64
35	42.47	46.68
36	41.54	45.72
37	40.61	44.76
38	39.68	43.81
39	38.76	42.86
40	37.84	41.91
41	36.93	40.97
42	36.02	40.03
43	35.12	39.1
44	34.22	38.17
45	33.33	37.24
46	32.45	36.32
47	31.57	35.41
48	30.71	34.5
49	29.84	33.59
50	28.99	32.69
51	28.15	31.8
52	27.32	30.91
53	26.49	30.02
54	25.68	29.14

Exact Age	Male Life Expectancy	Female Life Expectancy
55	24.87	28.27
56	24.06	27.4
57	23.26	26.53
58	22.48	25.67
59	21.69	24.82
60	20.92	23.97
61	20.16	23.14
62	19.4	22.31
63	18.66	21.49
64	17.92	20.69
65	17.19	19.89
66	16.48	19.1
67	15.77	18.32
68	15.08	17.55
69	14.4	16.79
70	13.73	16.05
71	13.08	15.32
72	12.44	14.61
73	11.82	13.91
74	11.21	13.22
75	10.62	12.55
76	10.04	11.9
77	9.48	11.26
78	8.94	10.63
79	8.41	10.03
80	7.9	9.43
81	7.41	8.86
82	6.94	8.31
83	6.49	7.77

Exact Age	Male Life Expectancy	Female Life Expectancy
84	6.06	7.26
85	5.65	6.77
86	5.26	6.31
87	4.89	5.87
88	4.55	5.45
89	4.22	5.06
90	3.92	4.69
91	3.64	4.36
92	3.38	4.04
93	3.15	3.76
94	2.93	3.5
95	2.75	3.26
96	2.58	3.05
97	2.44	2.87
98	2.3	2.7
99	2.19	2.54
100	2.07	2.39
101	1.96	2.25
102	1.85	2.11
103	1.75	1.98
104	1.66	1.86
105	1.56	1.74
106	1.47	1.62
107	1.39	1.52
108	1.3	1.41
109	1.22	1.31
110	1.15	1.22
111	1.07	1.13
112	1	1.05

Exact Age	Male Life Expectancy	Female Life Expectancy
113	0.94	0.97
114	0.87	0.89
115	0.81	0.82
116	0.75	0.75
117	0.7	0.7
118	0.64	0.64
119	0.59	0.59

Source: Social Security Administration, www.socialsecurity.gov/OACT/STATS/ table4c6.html

SOCIAL SECURITY PLANNING RESOURCES

Where Can I Go for Help?

The complexities of Social Security are a mystery even to many financial advisors, attorneys, and CPAs. In fact, some of the more advanced strategies we cover in this book—strategies that regularly increase lifetime Social Security benefits by more than $100,000—are a mystery even to many Social Security Administration employees!

The Social Security Administration (SSA) is not set up to help retirees make the best decision regarding their benefits. SSA personnel are prohibited from dispensing advice. They are trained to help you get the highest benefit you can walk out with *that day*— not the highest benefit your entire family can get *over the course of your entire life*. They also cannot help you with any of the tax considerations or, most importantly, how it interacts with your other sources of income and assets.

So where can you turn?

If there is a single overriding message we hope comes across in this book, it's that maximizing Social Security benefits as part of an overall strategy for making your money last in retirement is *not* as simple as it may seem. If you are not comfortable assessing all of your options on your own, it is important to have a knowledgeable financial advisor help you chart the right road to help you achieve your fiscal goals in retirement because the rules of that road are constantly changing.

That said, we nonetheless believe there are some things you can and should do in preparation for meeting with your financial advisor to become savvier. One of them, of course, is reading this book. But there are some other helpful resources available to you as well.

It's often been said that a little knowledge can be a dangerous thing. But where your personal finances are concerned, the more knowledge you have and the more actively involved you are in planning for your financial future, the more successful the collaboration between you and your financial advisor is likely to be.

Here are some additional resources for information on Social Security benefits and retirement issues that we recommend to you in preparation for that all-important meeting with your advisor:

Calculating Longevity

- Living to 100 (www.livingto100.com) uses the most current and carefully researched medical and scientific data in order to estimate how long you will live.
- Society of Actuaries (www.soa.org/research/software-tools/research-simple-life-calculator.aspx) uses your choice of either Social Security Life Expectancy or the Annuity 2000 table life expectancy to provide estimates.

Retirement Issues and Social Security Planning

- America's Wealth Management Show with Dean Barber (www.americaswealthmanagementshow.com) includes a free calculator to find out how much you stand to gain by making the right choice for claiming benefits.

- Social Security Timing (www.socialsecuritytiming.com) provides a calculator and also helps you find a local advisor to assist.
- Social Security Administration (www.socialsecurity.gov or www.ssa.gov), the main site and central home page for the U.S. government's Social Security Administration.
- Social Security Administration (www.socialsecurity.gov/ retire2) for information on delaying benefits.
- Social Security Administration (www.ssa.gov/planners/ benefitcalculators.htm) to access Social Security's free Retirement Estimator to determine benefits based on your earnings record. Keep in mind that these are only estimates. Social Security cannot supply your actual benefit amount until you apply for benefits.

Publications

The following brochures are available from the Social Security Administration at their website www.ssa.gov/pubs. Search each by title or number. Many are available in audio versions and in printable form in various languages such as Spanish, Farsi, Vietnamese, Polish, Russian, and Arabic.

- On *Retirement Benefits*, Social Security Administration: Publication No. 05-10035
- On *Disability Benefits*, Social Security Administration: Publication No. 05-10029
- On *How Work Affects Your Benefits*, Social Security Administration: Publication No. 05-10069
- On *Social Security and Taxes (Government Pension Offset)*, Social Security Administration: Publication No. 05-10007 for government workers who may be eligible for Social Security benefits on the earnings record of a spouse

- On *Windfall Elimination Provision*, Social Security Administration: Publication No. 05-10045 for people who worked in another country or government workers who also are eligible for their own Social Security benefits
- On *Tax Information for Older Americans*, Internal Revenue Service: Publication 554 and *Social Security Benefits and Equivalent Railroad Retirement Benefits*, Publication 915 (available at www.irs.gov/publications)

Toll-Free Numbers

- Internal Revenue Service: 1-800-829-3676
- Social Security Administration: 1-800-772-1213 or 1-800-325-0778 (if you are deaf or hard of hearing)

MY LIVING EXPENSES WORKSHEET

My Necessary and Discretionary Living Expenses

	Monthly	Annually
HOUSING		
Mortgage or rent		
Second mortgage or rent		
Phone		
Electricity		
Gas		
Water and sewer		
Cable		
Waste removal		
Maintenance or repairs		
Supplies		
Other		
Subtotals		
TRANSPORTATION		
Vehicle 1 payment		
Vehicle 2 payment		
Bus/taxi fare		
Insurance		
Licensing		
Fuel		
Maintenance		
Other		
Subtotals		

	Monthly	**Annually**
INSURANCE		
Home		
Health		
Life		
Other		
Subtotals		
FOOD		
Groceries		
Dining out		
Other		
Subtotals		
CHILDREN		
Medical		
Clothing		
School tuition		
School supplies		
Organization dues or fees		
Lunch money		
Child care		
Toys/games		
Other		
Subtotals		
PETS		
Food		
Medical		
Grooming		
Toys		
Other		
Subtotals		

	Monthly	**Annually**
PERSONAL CARE		
Medical		
Hair/nails		
Clothing		
Dry cleaning		
Health club		
Organization dues or fees		
Other		
Subtotals		

ENTERTAINMENT		
Video/DVD		
CDs/Downloads		
Movies		
Concerts		
Sporting events		
Live theater		
Other		
Subtotals		

LOANS		
Personal		
Student		
Credit card		
Credit card		
Credit card		
Other		
Subtotals		

	Monthly	**Annually**
TAXES		
Federal		
State		
Local		
Other		
Subtotals		
SAVINGS OR INVESTMENTS		
Retirement account		
Investment account		
College		
Other		
Subtotals		
GIFTS AND DONATIONS		
Charity 1		
Charity 2		
Charity 3		
Subtotals		
LEGAL		
Attorney		
Alimony		
Payments on lien or judgment		
Other		
Subtotals		
	Monthly	**Annually**
Totals		

ABOUT THE AUTHORS

DEAN BARBER, RFC

Dean Barber, founder and president of Barber Financial Group, began his career in the financial services industry on one of the bleakest days in recent history, October 19, 1987, Black Monday.

It didn't take him long to realize that the answer doesn't lie in how much money a person makes; it's in how much they keep. He has built one of Kansas City's premier financial management firms, focusing on assisting retirees, pre-retirees, and business owners in building and preserving their wealth through the concepts of asset management, tax strategies, and estate planning.

Dean has become nationally known for his financial planning advice. Since 2003, he has hosted a (now nationally) syndicated radio program, *America's Wealth Management Show*. He has been a regular contributor to many publications and broadcasts such as *The Wall Street Journal, Fox Business News, CNBC*, www.Bankrate.com, the *International Business Times, U.S. News & World Report, Forbes, Small Business CEO Magazine*, www.NYTimes.com, www.InvestmentNews.com, *Business Week*, www.Portfolio.com, *Kansas City Business Journal*, KMBC-9TV, and KSHB-41TV.

His weekly radio program features guests such as economist Harry Dent and Ed Slott, the CPA often quoted by *The Wall Street Journal*. He has also lectured and presented to key employees for several *Fortune 500* corporations.

He is a registered representative of National Planning Corporation (NPC), member FINRA and SIPC, as well as an Investment Advisor Representative of Barber Financial Group and NPC, both Registered Investment Advisors. NPC is separate from and unrelated to BFG and all other named entities. This is his second book.

Joe Elsasser, CFP®, RHU, REBC

Joe Elsasser is the Managing Partner of Sequent Planning LLC, a Registered Investment Advisor located in Omaha, Nebraska. He has been involved in the insurance and financial services industry since 2001 as an advisor, a marketer, and a coach.

A Certified Financial Planner (CFP®), Registered Health Underwriter (RHU), Registered Employee Benefits Consultant (REBC), licensed Investment Advisor Representative, and licensed insurance agent, Joe helps prospective retirees maximize the inevitable tradeoffs between social insurance programs such as Social Security and Medicare, insurance options, such as long-term care, life insurance and annuities, investment options such as stocks, bonds, mutual funds, exchange traded funds, and a variety of alternative investment options in light of tax and estate planning concerns.

He has been quoted or featured in various publications including *US News & World Report, USA Today, The Wall Street Journal, Kiplinger,* and *Money,* and he has been interviewed on PBS stations. He is also the creator of Social Security Timing®, a software package that helps advisors identify optimal Social Security claiming strategies for their clients.

For information on booking authors Dean Barber or Joe Elsasser as keynote speakers for your next conference, meeting, or company event, or to order additional copies of *Social Security Essentials* for your employees and/or clients, please contact their respective offices:

Dean Barber

Barber Financial Group
Office: (913) 393-1000
Toll-Free: (888) 848-8003
info@barberfinancialgroup.com
www.BarberFinancialGroup.com

Joe Elsasser

Social Security Timing
Office: (402) 343-3654
Toll-Free: (877) 844-7213
jelsasser@socialsecuritytiming.com
www.SocialSecurityTiming.com

INDEX

S

Made in the USA
Charleston, SC
24 September 2013